The Three Word Brief

Simple Advice for People Who Advertise

Bob Hoffman

The Three Word Brief by Bob Hoffman

Cover Design: Jeff Goodby
Publisher: Type A Group, LLC
For information contact: bob@typeagroup.com

ISBN 9798343789638

Also by Bob Hoffman

101 Contrarian Ideas About Advertising

Marketers Are From Mars, Consumers Are From New Jersey

BadMen

Laughing@Advertising

Advertising For Skeptics

Adscam

AUDIO BOOK

The Simple Art of Advertising - or - How to Stop Complicating the

Shit Out of Everything

Praise for Bob

"FASCINATING… AN EYE-OPENING BOOK" - Kirkus Reviews

"FABULOUSLY IRREVERENT" – *Time, Inc*

"CAUSTIC YET TRUTHFUL" – *The Wall Street Journal*

"THE MOST PROVOCATIVE MAN IN ADVERTISING" – *Fuel Lines*

"SAVAGE CRITIQUES OF DIGITAL HYPE" – *Financial Times*

"IT'S NICE TO FIND A REAL THINKER IN THE AD BUSINESS THESE DAYS" – *Jack Trout, Forbes*

"BOB IS THE LITTLE CHILD WHO POINTS OUT THAT THE EMPEROR IS WEARING NO CLOTHES … I'M JEALOUS. I WISH I'D BEEN BRAVE ENOUGH TO BE THIS RUDE."
– *Prof. Byron Sharp, author, "How Brands Grow"*

"'ONE OF OUR TRULY GREAT MARKETING ICONOCLASTS"
– *Mark Ritson*

"BOB HOFFMAN…IS POSSIBLY GOING TO BE SEEN AS THE MOST INFLUENTIAL PERSON OF THE DECADE WHEN IT COMES TO MEDIA" – *Tom Denford, CEO, ID Comms*

"HOFFMAN IS A VOICE OF REASON IN OUR INCREASINGLY CRAZY WORLD OF ADVERTISING. HIS NO BULLSHIT, DOWN-TO EARTH REASONING WILL HAVE YOU RE-EXAMINIING EVERYTHING YOU DO." - *MediaPost*

For Fig

INTRODUCTION

Nothing human works as advertised.

I'm astonished when people are surprised at the failures of capitalism, or socialism, or communism. I'm amazed when people are stunned that Democratic policies don't work. Or Republican policies. Or liberal policies, or conservative policies. I'm astounded when people express dismay that corporations are stupid, or government is wasteful.

I laugh when I hear people complain that economists were wrong, or that an education scheme didn't pan out, or that a social policy had the opposite of its intended effect. How much history do you have to read until you realize that there is no perfectly right way to do things, just different wrong ways? How many failures does it take to realize that systems devised by humans never seem to work as advertised? The longer a system survives, the more obvious its flaws become. It's like the slight wobble of a top. The longer it spins the worse it gets. The best we can do is to identify the systems that wobble the least.

We exist in a world of delusions.

Our delusions live inside us and color everything we do. They infect our opinions of who we are. They distort our place in the world, twist our behaviors, and warp our sense of reality. Like the proverbial fish in the ocean, we are so immersed in delusions we can't even sense they are there. We are very good at filtering out information that does not fit neatly into our vision of the world. *"We can't cope otherwise"* says James Glieck, author of *Chaos* (and the famous 'butterfly effect'), *Genius*, and *The Information*.

The business of advertising is particularly rife with delusions. We think we know how advertising works. We think we know what will motivate people and what will not. And yet every day we unconsciously filter out compelling evidence that we don't really know much at all. After months of research and testing we create advertising that has little or even no effect. After hundreds of thousand of dollars in development we launch websites that no one ever bothers with. And yet we continue.

We go into presentations and make bold, cocksure statements about our own particular brand of delusional advertising philosophy. And we never have the guts or self- assurance to tell the truth -- that all our posturing is just an estimate of likelihoods and a speculation on probabilities.

Part of it is our fault. We are not willfully deceitful. We just find it very hard to admit that we are devoting so much of our energy and our soul to something about which we really understand so little. Part of it is the environment. Marketers want results. They don't want to hear that they are spending tens of millions of dollars on likelihoods and probabilities. They want results and they want them now.

Advertising is chock full of contingencies and unintended effects. There are a multitude of critical steps in the development of advertising. None of which assures success. Every one of which can foreshadow failure. Something as routine as the casting of an actor can have an enormous effect on the success or failure of a campaign. And that is just one of dozens of weighty variables.

We cannot possibly assess all the variables in a methodical way. So we fall back on our prejudices and our mathematical models of how advertising works. In other words, we call forth our delusions.

The workings of the real world are impossibly complex and messy. And in advertising, as in every other human endeavor, as Glieck says, we *"prefer to turn a blind eye to reality's messiness."*

AUTHOR'S NOTES

I spent over forty years in the advertising business. That makes me an expert on exactly nothing.

It did, however, afford me the opportunity to develop some firmly-held (and some would say, ill-informed) opinions about the craft of advertising. After I left the ad business I spent several years writing about it. Consequently I have a lot of words that, if properly arranged, might constitute a helpful book.

There are many people - CEO's, CFO's, entrepreneurs, business owners - who have to make decisions about advertising but have no formal training or experience in the field. So I decided to go through my oeuvre (fancy French word for 'pile of stuff') and pick out pieces that might be of most value to a civilian, untrained in advertising, who has to make ad decisions. I also added in new pieces which might be useful.

Unlike most advertising and marketing books, this one won't have too many charts, graphs, case histories or data. It will mostly feature the comprehensive musings of a skeptical old duffer trying desperately to evolve a sensible explanation for the chaos he senses has overtaken our industry.

I also have to admit that I have very little confidence that many people formally trained in advertising know what the hell they're doing. Which is why so much advertising is so awful and ineffectual. So to the people who have gone to 'ad school' or received an MBA and have been force fed a whole lot of horseshit about advertising, this might be helpful to you, too.

The first part of this book is called "Impressionism" and is mostly about the *creation* of advertising. Part two is called "Inside The Black Box" and is about the *distribution* of advertising. Specifically, it is about how the dominant form of contemporary advertising — programmatic online advertising — is part advertising, part con game, and part criminal enterprise that is probably robbing advertisers of hundreds of billions of dollars every year. The third part is called "Mktg Stinx" and contains some items I've written about the foibles, failures and fecklessness of traditional marketing practice.

You will quickly notice that most of the content of this book is in conflict with contemporary marketing and advertising 'best practices.' That's because 'best practices' is just a pleasanter way of saying 'what all the other shitheads are doing.' If you want to do what everyone else is doing, I suggest you return this book immediately and get your money back.

Table of Contents

Introduction
Author's Notes
PART ONE: IMPRESSIONISM

The Three Word Brief
Advertising As Impressionism
Einstein on Advertising
Kings, Popes, & Advertisers
Marketers and Improv
Luxury of Strategy
Data Is Mud
Improving Things To Death
Advertising's First Responders
The Human Factor
Our Principle Problem
Philosophy or Donuts?
Advertising Is a Weak Force
Are Creative Ads More Effective?
Tyranny of Strategy
Ego and Failure
Let's Do It On The Floor
Reality at the DMV
You've Got a Brand Problem
The Most Powerful Force in Marketing
Storytelling or Personalization. Pick One
The Handsomest Man In The World
Sidewalk Psychologists
Road to Reality
Public Advertising vs Private Advertising

What if Precision Targeting Doesn't Work?
Advertising's Untold Stories
Prisoners of Youth
Advertising Is Like Exercise
Beware of Marketers with Ideologies
Monty Python and Associates
Great Advertising Is the Best Strategy
And One More Thing

PART TWO: INSIDE THE BLACK BOX

Utopia
Understanding the Black Box
Disneyland for Crooks
Your Disappearing Money
Honey, Did You See My $140 Billion?
What is Ad Fraud?
How Large Is Ad Fraud?
Why Is Ad Fraud Thriving?
Programmatic Poop Funnel
Enormous Demand for Garbage
Billions of Mistakes. No One Noticed
The Google/YouTube Scandal
Forbes' Con Job
World's Clumsiest Cover-Up
Worldwide Hackathon
Perfecting Incompetence
Conspiracy of Silence
How to Protect Yourself
My Talk at the EU Parliament

PART THREE: MKTG STINX

Dyspeptic Skeptic
Marketers Are From Mars, Consumers Are From New Jersey
Glossary of Marketing
Robbie & Ruthie Talk About Pickles
Stop Branding
Is It Art or Science?

Women With Their Shirts Off
The Restaurant for People Who Don't Like Food
Life in Conferenceland
Legend of Marketing Man
Simplifiers and Complicators
Industrialization of Advertising
Sell More Shit
Asking the Wrong Questions
The Invisible Advertising Awards
Advertising's Hidden Enemy
Creativity Without Talent
Here's To The Bobbleheads
The Existential Adman
No Wonder Mktg Stinx
Acknowledgements
About The Author

Bob Hoffman

Part One

IMPRESSIONISM

The Three Word Brief

Those of us who create advertising or make advertising decisions need to start from a position of reality. What can advertising realistically achieve and how can we best achieve it?

Advertising is a small part of marketing. We advertisers don't control the product. We don't control the pricing. We don't control the sales force, the distribution, the customer service or the business strategy. The only thing we control is one aspect of communication.

Which leads to a big question. What is the one capability of advertising that has the greatest likelihood of resulting in success? Is it creativity? Is it differentiation? Is it positioning? Is it precision targeting? Is it empathy? Is it brand purpose? Is it salience (whatever that means.) Or is it something else?

The correct answer is, it's something else. But until we know what that something else is, our objective is not clear and our task is not well-defined.

Before launching a new campaign marketers, branding experts, and advertising practitioners often spend months trying to define what a brand should stand for. We are very fond of the concept of 'brand meaning.' This is driven by the belief that consumers impute specific attributes to brands and exercise their buying prerogatives based on the meaning they assign to the brand, and how well that meaning aligns with their personal needs or values.

Marketers also believe that consumers want to have relationships with brands, and be part of a brand's 'tribe' or community, and co-create with brands and, of course, respect and trust their brand's purpose. I think this is all largely horseshit.

The idea that the brands we use are intensely important to us and that we spend time and energy sussing out their meaning and trustworthiness is a deeply ingrained marketing fantasy. For most people, their relationship with most of the brands they buy is shallow, transactional, and contingent. Brands are not nearly as important or meaningful as we marketers would like them to be.

Are there some brands we're attached to? Sure. We each have a handful. But consumers are faced with thousands of brands. The likelihood of yours being one of the handful they are strongly attached to is absurdly small.

Whenever I argue that brands are not as important to consumers as we marketers think they are, I get the same response from traditional marketers: *"Oh, yeah, well how about Apple and Nike...?"* I call this arguing from the extreme. They take the most extreme version of something and pretend it's the norm. Of course, there are a handful of brands - like Apple - that have very loyal customers to whom the brand may be very meaningful. These handful of brands are two or three standard deviations from normal and, I'm sorry, but your brand ain't one of them.

Consumers are annoyingly impervious to understanding the finer points of product positioning, differentiation, and brand meaning. Don't agree? Stop someone on the street today and ask them what the difference is between BMW and Mercedes-Benz? Ask them for the difference between Coke and Pepsi? Ask them how Nike is different from Adidas? I will bet you very large sums of money that their responses will have little to no correlation to the strategic documents floating around those brands' headquarters. And these are some of the most successful brands in the world.

Each of these brands has spent billions of dollars over the years concocting delusions of differentiation. They believe their brands are successful because of their unique brand meaning. They're wrong.

The main advertising influence on their success is *fame* — the creation of fame and the maintenance of fame. As you'll see, I believe the most powerful contribution to brand success that advertising confers is fame. Not brand meaning, or relationship building, or brand purpose or any of the other fantasies that the advertising and marketing industry has concocted. Fame is just one reason for their success, but it is the primary contribution advertising has made.

Here are some questions:

- Why do some actors get million dollar fees for appearing in movies while other equally good actors get nothing?

- Why do some people get the best tables at fancy restaurants while nicer people can't even get in?

- Why do some people *always* get a call back when they leave a phone message and you don't?

Right, because they're famous. Fame is a massive advantage in business and in life.

Simple ideas like fame are anathema to the marketing industry. We advertising and marketing professionals make our living by convincing business people that marketing communication is a deeply mystifying and specialized practice that requires particular knowledge and acumen. So we do our best to complicate the shit out of it.

That's one of the reasons why 'brand meaning' is such a popular idea. The more mysterious we can make brand building, the more brands need people like us to interpret consumer psychology. Brand meaning fits the bill very nicely.

But if the contribution advertising makes to consumer buying behavior is more reliably traceable to familiarity than to brand meaning, who needs all the relentless, expensive busywork we throw at developing brand meaning? How much value does all our research, ethnography, strategy and planning have if actual consumer behavior is more directly aligned to simple familiarity than to the meaning of the brand? Or its position? Or its purpose? Or any of the other esoteric contributions advertising is purported to make?

The people who promote the importance of brand meaning are promulgating a self- serving theory that puts them at the center of marketing activity by placing the interpretation of consumer behavior in their hands. But let's play devil's advocate for a moment and give the brand meaning crowd the benefit of the doubt. Let's stipulate that consumers impute specific attributes to brands and buy based on how well a brand's meaning aligns with their needs or values. Then the question becomes how much of brand's 'meaning' is contributed by advertising as opposed to all the other inputs consumer's get — like word of mouth; the reports of friends; the recommendations of experts; the retail experience; the reviews of critics; the look and feel of the product; the cultural landscape; and a thousand other influences floating around that advertising can't control or influence.

Ironically, the brand meaning crowd tend to be further removed from the behavior of actual consumers than they'd have us believe. They claim to 'understand the consumer,' but do they? First of all, there is no such thing as 'the consumer.' All there are are people.

Next, it has been demonstrated time and again that marketing and advertising people live in a world that is only tangentially related to the world of most of the people they are trying to influence. If you doubt this, I will be happy to accompany you to the DMV and show you what your customers actually look like.

Marketing executives' understanding of consumers is usually not based on actual first-hand experience, but on the reports of people who brief them — researchers, strategists, and planners. The researchers, strategists, and planners tend to share the same brand delusions that the marketing people have. When you're looking for brand meaning, it's very rare not to find it.

Try this. Read the documents that your researchers, strategists, and planners have written about the meaning of your brand. Then get out in the street and ask a few people what comes to mind about your brand. I promise, you'll be appalled.

While most brands do not have deep meaning to most of us, and while our discernment of brand positioning and differentiation may not be all it's cracked up to be, at some point when people are buying they have to make a decision. It is not that positioning and differentiation are irrelevant. It's that *a)* they are not advertising's primary contribution to brand success and *b)* they are not as compelling to real people as most marketers think they are.

Nonetheless, when we are creating advertising, it has to be about something. Positioning and differentiation are better than non-positioning and non-differentiation. So go ahead and position and differentiate away. Just don't fool yourself into believing that they are advertising's central goal.

Oh yeah, and don't ever let some half-assed marketer's idea of meaning, purpose, empathy, empowerment, positioning, differentiation (or whatever happens to be the brand babbler cliché of the month) get in the way of a great idea. In an environment like advertising, where strategic insight is usually a cruel joke, a great creative idea is usually the best advertising strategy.

I'm sorry to have to say this out loud, but I suspect you probably know it's true — much of what goes on in ad agencies and marketing departments is busywork. It's needless meetings about worthless memos and worthless memos about needless meetings. Sure, every now and then someone comes up with a unique ad strategy but most of the brilliant strategies that appear in the lore of advertising weren't brilliant strategies at all. They were great creative ideas that were reverse engineered to appear to have been the result of brilliant strategy.

The questionable brand 'differentiators' dreamed up in conference rooms and codified in briefing documents are largely lost on consumers and play secondary roles in most actual purchasing behavior. To real people, the competing products in most categories are remarkably similar. And yet developing so-called brand differentiators — through research, ethnography, strategy and planning exercises — occupy an enormous amount of time, energy, and money. If you've had a look at advertising lately, I doubt I have to tell you how infrequently they result in anything very compelling.

Brands that are well-known and distinctive in their categories - the great contribution that advertising can make - are the ones that tend to have the most marketing success and tend to be category leaders.

Is this always the case? No. Is it the most probable case? Yes. Nothing in marketing is absolute, all we have are likelihoods and probabilities.

Marketers have the naive but apparently fact-resistant belief that customers care deeply about what they buy, and buy according to a logical or emotional comparison of what they want and what the brand says it's 'about.' Sometimes they do. But mostly they don't. I am officially skeptical that consumers exercise as much conscious assessment of alternatives when they make most purchases as we marketers believe.

- Do people recognize the differences between brands? *Not as much as we'd like to believe.*
- Do people have brand preferences? *In most cases, yes.*
- Does a strong brand have value to a marketer? *Without question, tremendous value.*

Q: Wait a second. You say consumers aren't that interested in brands but a strong brand has tremendous value. WTF?

A: Exactly. Most consumer choices are done without deep thought. People don't have the time, energy, or inclination to assess the ramifications of every brand decision before they buy. The fact that people are not as sensitive to brand differences as we think makes a strong brand *more powerful, not less.*

Ironically, the less energy people spend analyzing brand meaning, the more important familiarity (or as Prof. Sharp might call it, 'mental availability') becomes.

One more time: The less patience and appetite people have for analyzing brand variables, the more important brand familiarity and comfort become. Familiarity and comfort with a brand come in a variety of ways, including...the brand my mom used...the brand my friend uses and likes...the brand that works satisfactorily for me...the brand I hear about a lot...the brand I see everywhere.

Any non-ideological interpretation of consumer behavior can lead to only one conclusion: Most people buy most brands in most categories because they are familiar and comfortable with them. Not because they are the most deeply understood or the most personally meaningful. The leading brands in virtually every category tend to be the most familiar, regardless of what the brand babblers say about their meaning.

Let's make this even simpler. People are mostly too busy, too lazy, or too indifferent to give 2/5ths of a flying shit about the 'meaning' of the stuff they buy. Mostly, they buy on auto- pilot from familiar brands they feel comfortable with. The easier you make it for people to choose your brand the more likely you are to be successful. From the standpoint of advertising, the best way to make the choice easier is to be famous and let probability do its job.

This is true even for brands that are already famous. Like the man said, when you get the plane to 35,000 feet you don't turn off the engines. This is why outstanding creative work is such an unmatched advertising asset. It creates a lot more fame per dollar.

A brand that is famous has enormous advantages over its rival brands that are not famous. This does not mean that fame is a guarantee of success. Fame cannot save a stupid business idea or a stupid product. Fame is strong. But stupid is stronger.

There are several ways for brands to achieve fame. Some do it by being clearly superior and generating exceptional word of mouth. This is obviously the best way to become famous. Some get lucky. They're good copy and the media love to cover them and provide them with zillions in free exposure. Others become famous through imaginative PR initiatives, clever stunts, the charismatic personalities of their leaders, or a combination of these things. There are many ways to achieve fame, and they're all good.

The most expensive way to become famous is through advertising. It is the most expensive, but also the most reliable. It is the only avenue to fame that you can buy your way into.

If I was a CEO I'd call my agency into my office and give them a three word brief: *Make us famous.*

Advertising As Impressionism

The advertising industry has an incomplete idea of how advertising affects people. Traditionally we have described the elements of advertising impact as a blend of logic and emotion.

The case for logic suggests that consumer behavior is mostly rational. This idea (as first argued by Adam Smith) asserts that markets are rational and people behave rationally. They do not throw their money away on stupid crap. There is a lot of persuasive evidence for this model. A good example is in retailing. Retailers know that they can stimulate sales by lowering prices, offering discounts, and utilizing other types of promotional activities. This is clear evidence for a logical basis for some consumer behavior.

The case for emotion asserts that consumer behavior is largely non-rational. One basis for this theory, brilliantly demonstrated by Daniel Kahnemann, holds that people are not fully aware of their motivations and are often ruled by emotions. The evidence for this model is equally persuasive. I have previously written about the

Toyota Corolla that was the exact same vehicle as the Chevy Geo Prism, cost $1,500 more, yet outsold it 3 to 1.

In the prevailing theory of how advertising works there is presumably some balance of logic and emotion that will be best suited for purpose. In some cases a highly logical approach is preferable. In other cases a more emotional approach is best. This binary logic/emotion continuum is a false dichotomy that ignores a powerful and equally important factor. We'll get to that in a minute.

But first, let's talk about subatomic physics.

Quantum physics gives us a useful, if imperfect, analogy to what I am proposing. Before quantum theory, subatomic thingies were described as either particles or waves. Quantum theory taught us that under some circumstances a thingie might behave as a particle and under other circumstances it might behave as a wave. It provided a liquidity between particles and waves. You could choose to call it a particle or call it a wave, but whatever a human decided to call it was irrelevant. In reality it was still an imprecise, fluid, sub-atomic thingie. Sometimes a particle and sometimes a wave.

Einstein also helped us understand hidden equivalencies. His famous equation $E=mc^2$ taught us that mass and energy, which seemed to be two different things, were actually two manifestations of the same thing. Depending on its energy state, it could appear as mass, or it could appear as energy. Underneath it all, it was the same stuff.

I would like to propose that 'impressionism theory' can give us a similar liquid insight into how advertising works.

Consumers are not logic machines, nor are they puppy dogs. Our traditional belief that logic and emotion are two different and separate things is insufficient. Our belief that advertising's effect on consumers is some amalgam of logic and emotion is also insufficient. Let's look at an example.

Dave Trott has written about an incident in which Charles Saatchi was searching for an idea for a poster to convince people to cover their food so flies wouldn't spread germs to it. Saatchi was rifling through material on the subject when he came across some old leaflets. According to Trott...

One of the leaflets had this written in it:

This is what happens when a fly lands on your food.

Flies can't eat solid food, so to soften it up they vomit on it.

Then they stamp the vomit in until it's a liquid (usually stamping in a few germs for good measure).

Then when it's good and runny they suck it all back up again, probably dropping some excrement at the same time.

And then, when they've finished eating, it's your turn.

Saatchi said "That's it, don't change a word, that's the poster.'"

This is an excellent example of a logical argument that undoubtedly generates an emotional response. It shows us clearly that logic and emotion are not so distinctly different as we might think. In fact it is highly likely that logical arguments can lead to emotional reactions, and vice versa. You might choose to call a reaction to this story logical or you might choose to call it emotional. But underlying whatever you call it is one undeniable fact - it created a strong impression. The *impression* was the primary asset that was delivered.

The processing that goes into a buying decision is imprecise. We have chosen to describe it as some combination of logic and emotion. While both may be relevant, this description is not comprehensive. The ultimate product of advertising may sometimes be a logical conclusion or it may sometimes be an emotional feeling, but it is always an *impression*.

Advertising creates an impression whether you intend it to or not. That impression may be strong and positive, or weak and meaningless. The power of that impression is related to the skill with which it is delivered.

Both the logic model and the emotion model, while intellectually attractive, have unpleasant side effects. The idea that advertising must present logical benefits has lead to a catalog of truly horrifying ads based on what I refer to as the 'court case' framework in which 'our-brand-is-better-than-their-brand-because' is the underlying structure. The idea that advertising must engender emotion has also lead to painfully awful ads featuring instantly forgettable vignettes of Grandpa and Timmy fishing, or birthday surprises at the old folks home.

But a theory of advertising based on the strength of impressions leads us away from those traps. It leads us to a model of advertising in which the power of the delivery of the impression takes precedence over the false dichotomy of logic and emotion.

One of the primary drivers of impressionism in advertising is aesthetics. Some might call it entertainment value, or subjective appeal, or creativity. Aesthetic elements of advertising may include design, language, production, casting, performance, and music. Aesthetics create a liquidity between logic and emotion.

The powerful impression that was created by the 'fly' example above was driven by the language that was used by the writer. Underlying a logical argument about cleanliness there was an aesthetic element that transformed logic into emotion -- it created liquidity between logic and emotion -- and the result was a powerful impression.

Aesthetics wash over both logic and emotion and either elevate or diminish the strength of both. Aesthetics are the third leg of the advertising stool and are a powerful driver of the impressionistic nature of advertising.

Neither logic nor emotion is an adequate explanation for the advertising power of a Nike swoosh or a drum-playing gorilla. But impressionism is.

I am obviously not the first to recognize the importance of aesthetics in advertising. But somehow in the literature of our industry we have condensed the effect of advertising into a right-brain/left-brain dichotomy and we have not derived a whole-brain theory. I am choosing to call this whole-brain theory 'impressionism.'

Impressionism theory will be very unpopular with CMOs and MBAs. These people can point to logical advertising solutions as indicators of their analytic abilities. They can point to emotional solutions as proof of their credentials as sidewalk psychologists. But impressionism, by its very nature, is imprecise. The whole point of impressionism is to be imprecise. Marketers will have a tough time explaining to their egos or to their bosses the value of impressionism.

Marketers prefer precise answers that are wrong to imprecise answers that are right.

Just as quantum theory resolved the conundrum of particles and waves in physics, I believe impressionism theory may resolve the conundrum of the logic/emotion straightjacket in advertising.

There has been a lot of hand-wringing in the marketing community about the state of creativity in advertising. I may be kidding myself, but I believe impressionism theory may open a window to a more undogmatic and supple definition of what constitutes effective advertising.

Einstein on Advertising

Albert Einstein was a pretty smart guy.

What most people don't know about Einstein is that in addition to uncovering the laws of relativity, the equivalency of mass and energy, and predicting that the speed of light was constant, he also said -- without knowing it -- one of the smartest things ever said about advertising.

After his amazing successes as a young man, Einstein spent the rest of his life searching for what was called the 'grand unified theory' -- a theory that would unify all the forces of nature including gravity, electro-magnetism, the strong and weak nuclear forces. Many physicists believed that these four forces must be different manifestations of one underlying force.

Einstein worked for forty years on this problem and failed in his attempts to uncover a grand unified theory. To date, no one has found it, and things have gotten even more confused with the conjectures about dark energy and dark matter.

Near the end of his life Einstein was being interviewed. The interviewer asked Einstein if he thought a grand unified theory would ever be found. He said, *"The answer to this problem, when found, will be simple."*

There's a lesson in there for us. No matter how complex a marketing or advertising problem may appear to be; no matter how much research has been done; no matter how many account planning insights have been concocted; no matter how many MBAs are complicating the shit out of it; no matter how many 100-page decks have been written, and Powerpoint presentations have been made, remember what Uncle Albert said -- the correct idea, when found, will be simple.

Kings, Popes, & Advertisers

Picture two fat old men in their underwear sitting on a park bench explaining to passersby that God wants everyone to do what they say.

Hold that image. We'll get back to it in a minute. Meanwhile...

Having spent more decades than is healthy in advertising, my view is that it is a fascinating business. What makes advertising fascinating is that to be good at it you have to understand one of the most incomprehensible of subjects —people.

To acquire an understanding of how people actually work requires a skill that most advertisers and marketers don't possess. It requires the ability to step away from the subject and see the big patterns of human behavior that are often hidden in plain sight.

In the modern era of humanity (let's say the last 2,000 years) the two most powerful institutions of human invention have been religion and government. The success of these institutions is generally presumed to be the result of either the power of their ideas or the power of the sword. I would like to add a third factor. I believe the success of religion and government owe much more to the creative arts than is generally recognized or acknowledged. Creative people - writers, artists, designers, musicians, architects - have played a critical role in legitimizing religious and political authority.

Let's get back to that initial image. Imagine a pope and a king sitting on a park bench without their costumes, trying to convince people to do what they say. All you have is two old men in their underwear spinning ridiculous fairy tales. Other than point and giggle, no one would pay them the slightest attention. But dress them up in glorious costumes, put them in a cathedral or a palace, surround them with beautiful art, beautiful music, and beautiful objects, re-work their fairy tales into lovely stories and suddenly you are tempted to believe.

Christianity began its life as a fringe movement within Judaism. While Judaism barely survived as a religious institution, Christianity swept over the western world. Christianity had enormous advantages over Judaism. One of which was that it was very adept at harnessing the power of artistry. For about a thousand years you could not make a living as a musician, a painter, a designer, a writer or an architect unless you did your work for the church. The western world's most creative minds dedicated their efforts to beautifying and glorifying Christianity. They were enormously successful. Some of the most beautiful music, art, structures, stories, and costumes the world has ever seen have been created in the service of religion.

As religious power started to ebb and migrate into secular hands — you might call it the separation of church and state — kings and queens began to vie with the clergy for the services of creative artists. The powerful imagery of palaces, costumes, music and art were employed by aristocratic political entities. For centuries average, undistinguished people, dressed up in fancy costumes, living in opulent environments, surrounded by beautiful objects and glorified in splendid tales were able to maintain secular rule — often unchallenged except by each other.

It would be comforting to believe that these people derived their power and authority from some form of transcendent wisdom or virtue. Sadly, history is perfectly clear on this. Kings and spiritual leaders have been every bit as flawed and ignorant as you and I.

Very ordinary people shrouded in extraordinary beauty have been able to maintain control of our most powerful institutions. The power of artistry in creating the perception of holiness and authority is so strong that over the centuries millions have been willing to give their lives for the glory of the most unexceptional of kings and spiritual leaders. I doubt that even the popes and kings recognized the role that aesthetics played in bestowing the illusion of virtue and authority on them.

For twenty years or more, the advertising industry has been steadily devaluing the importance of aesthetics in our business in favor of rational and easily measurable characteristics. It ought to be clear to marketers that without the benefit of swords, harnessing the power of the creative arts is among the most effective ways to maintain relevance and market dominance.

But most marketers don't see it that way. They are under the delusion that their products are unique and can stand and thrive on the strength of their rational attributes -- their utility, their practical benefits, and their brand meaning. Very few understand the power of artistry in market competition.

When they are faced with the reality of deteriorating customer loyalty, marketers have a hard time understanding it. If they appreciated the role that aesthetics play they might recognize the powerful relationship between creativity, human connections, and market power.

Nothing lasts forever. But with the advantage of aesthetic distinction, mundane brands and products (and, by the way, sooner or later *all* brands and products become mundane) can achieve surprising levels of success and thrive far beyond their inherent life expectancy. Without creative inspiration, brands and products eventually deteriorate into fat old men in their underwear sitting on a park bench.

Marketers and Improv

One way to look at creativity is that it is a form of improvisation. Improv is the talent that enables someone to react to a situation in an unexpected way that leads to an exhilarating outcome.

Average musicians know their scales and know how to play a chart. Excellent musicians are different. They can improvise. They take the chart that everyone else has but create something different and interesting out of it. They can feel the music that's happening around them in a unique way that allows them to find a different and superior interpretation of their part.

The same is true in comedy. Perhaps you know a funny person. What does that person do? She takes the same experience you are having but sees it differently and creates something unexpectedly delightful with it.

The reason so much of marketing is uninspired is that marketers are not taught to improvise. They are taught 'truths.' They have learned their fundamentals and know all the right moves. They are encouraged to apply what they have been taught. They are not encouraged to make shit up.

If I may paraphrase Richard Feynman, the problem isn't that marketers aren't clever. It's that they're clever enough to understand what they've been taught, but not clever enough to *question* what they've been taught.

Problems occur when they are faced with unique situations (and, by the way, *every* marketing situation is unique.) In a perfect world they might be expected to understand when and how to throw away the playbook. But they have never been taught that,

Overwhelmingly the solution they revert to is one of the many they have learned. That is why you will receive 10 emails today offering you 20% off, but no brass bands will come marching down your street.

Improvisation requires a heightened awareness of what's going on around you and the ability to feel the seams. Strictly established patterns are the enemy of improvisation, but are the currency of most marketing activity. Having worked in the advertising and marketing industry for many years, I heard the same tired formulas over and over.

Improvising is not easy. Only the best can do it well. Sadly, not many in marketing even understand that they are allowed to do it at all.

Luxury of Strategy

Loudmouth adweasels like me are always going off on the need for advertisers to abandon their addiction to short-termism and focus their attention on the long-term imperative of building their brands.

There is impressive evidence that in the fullness of time marketers are better served if their budgets are more weighted toward brand building advertising and less weighted toward short- term promotional (so-called 'performance') advertising.

The problem with this is that for a great many marketers surviving this week is a more compelling issue than the promise of a magnificent brand three years from now. Many businesses simply can't afford to do advertising that doesn't deliver instant returns.

This is not just an unpleasant theory of business, it is a fact of life. Short term and long term imperatives are not always aligned. There are many things that are short-term necessities but are harmful in the long term.

The world would be a much happier, more reasonable place if all the things we are compelled to do today could conform to what we'd like for tomorrow. But, sadly, the world doesn't always work that way. We don't want to be complicit in the burning of fossil fuels but we have to get to work.

Tactics can often be a matter of life and death, while strategy can be a luxury. As heavyweight boxing champion Mike Tyson once said, *"Everyone has a strategy until they get hit."*

Having spent centuries in the ad business, one thing I learned is that when it's all on the line, the tactical always drives out the strategic. This is not only true in business -- it is true in life. When critical decisions have to be made, surviving today always trumps rainbows tomorrow.

One of the most powerful and unrecognized benefits of a successful brand is the financial wherewithal to support both short-term and brand advertising. Many businesses don't have the means to do this.

Strategy is the great advantage of the wealthy.

Data Is Mud

Data is a fancy word for information. But like so many fancy words, it has achieved a sacred position in the world of advertising and marketing jargon. It has joined the ranks of 'branding', 'engagement', 'content', 'blockchain', 'metaverse', 'conversation', 'NFTs' and 'purpose' in the revolving lexicon of marketing obsessions.

However, just because data is an obnoxiously overworked platitude, doesn't mean it's not valuable. Information is useful.

In order to make intelligent decisions data is clearly necessary. But the question for advertisers is, just how useful *is* it and is it worth all the time, effort, and money we spend on collecting, organizing and analyzing it?

An alarming amount of data is being collected by the marketing industry. How much of the data is actually being used productively?

According to the Harvard Business Review, *"Only 3% of Companies' Data Meets Basic Quality Standards"*

According to The Audiencer, *"Most experts agree that only about 5% of data is being used in a meaningful way."*

Also according to the Harvard Business Review, *"Studies show that knowledge workers waste up to 50% of time hunting for data, identifying and correcting errors, and seeking confirmatory sources for data they do not trust."*

So right away we have problems. Based on the above, we have to question whether the ubiquitous blather about 'data-driven advertising' is even real or just another trendy advertising talking point. But let's give the data ninjas the full benefit of the doubt and stipulate that all the data they collect is accurate, easily accessible, and useful. Here's the problem:

Does anyone really believe that Coke has data that Pepsi doesn't have?

Does anyone believe that Coors has data that Budweiser doesn't have?

Does anyone believe that Ford has data that Chevy doesn't?

I'd bet large sums that they all have about the same data. And if they don't, a few clicks or phone calls and they can order up any data they want (according to published reports, about 80% of data 'owned' by marketers arrives via third parties.)

In the real world, what exactly does data *itself* afford you? Largely, it affords you the prospect of information parity with your competitors. And in what universe is parity a dynamic growth strategy?

But there is some true value in data. The real value comes from extraordinary people who can analyze and interpret it in brilliant ways. Give the same reservoir of data to two different groups of people and you will likely get two very different interpretations of what it means and two very different recommendations on what to do about it.

In my career I had the opportunity to review market research (data pretending to be science) on a frequent basis. It was a rare experience to have the designer of the research extract anything uniquely valuable. And it was even rarer to have that person present an astute course of action based on a singular interpretation of that data.

If the quality of contemporary advertising is to be attributed to being data-driven, it's being driven right off a cliff.

But there *are* some unusual people who can make data live and breathe. They can look at data and see things that we can't. They can tell you what the data *really* means. They can synthesize a unique point of view on what to do about it. These people are very rare and they provide the true value that can be derived from data.

Of course, this is contrary to the current marketing obsession with accumulating *as much data as possible,* which provides the *illusion* of understanding things and lets you think you are generating 'data-driven advertising.' Regrettably, it's not that easy. It's not how much data you have that matters. It's the intelligence, talent, and imagination of the people analyzing and strategizing from it that matters.

Data is mud. Most people just fling it around. But some people build the Taj Mahal. It ain't the data that makes the difference, it's the humans.

Improving Things To Death

One of the dangers successful brands face is falling into the hands of a dumbass marketer.

Successful brands are usually created by an inscrutable recipe of hard work, good product ideas, luck, and competent marketing. After a period of success there is always a second (or fifth, or tenth) generation of marketing. Looking to make an impact, these new generations of marketing often make the same mistake. Before we get to that mistake, let's talk about baseball.

Until the designated hitter rule became universal, in Major League Baseball's National League, pitchers had to hit. They were very bad hitters. Not because they lacked athletic ability, but because they usually didn't hit much in high school, college, or minor leagues. Hitting major league pitching is indescribably hard. If you rarely hit as an amateur, hitting in the major leagues is a nightmare.

Because pitchers were such bad hitters, National League teams usually had between 3 and 5 automatic outs in every game they played. This is a significant hardship because in every 9-inning game you only get 27 outs.

But baseball people are smart. They didn't spend a lot of time trying to teach pitchers how to hit. Yes, they had them take some batting practice to keep their timing up, but they figured that there's a limited amount of time to be spent in training, and it's best spent improving a pitcher's pitching technique rather than his hitting technique. In other words, there's more benefit in improving what he does *well* than in trying to improve what he does *badly*. Many marketers don't understand this.

Every company has strengths and weaknesses. The temptation to focus immoderate amounts of time, energy, and money on tweaking weaknesses rather than maximizing strengths can be overwhelming.

For many years I did advertising work for McDonald's. Marketing execs and other leaders at large corporations like this often don't last long. In my 16 years in their stable of agencies, I lived through several executive regimes. As each new regime took control it was inevitable that they would look at research and discover that - surprise! - the company did not score well with consumers on healthfulness. Of course not. They're a frigging fast food company. Who the hell goes to McDonald's for healthy food? Nonetheless, whenever new leadership showed up it was a pretty good bet that the wild goose chase would begin.

Instead of focusing on improving what they could do well and try to deliver better food in a cleaner store in less time, the new guys would go on a "let's pretend we're healthy" kick which would go nowhere. Months (sometimes years) of work and zillions of dollars would be wasted because time and money spent on making the bad a little less bad was not spent on making the good a little better.

In short, when new marketing leadership shows up at a successful brand, it is highly likely that the very first thing they will do is try to identify what "the problems" are. It makes them seem smart. If left unchecked this inevitably leads to obsessing over what the company does poorly instead of optimizing what the company does well.

In other words, they try to turn pitchers into hitters.

Another manifestation of dumbass "improvement" marketing is the frequent inability of marketing execs to leave successful things alone. This may be the least understood and most under-appreciated of marketing skills.

There is convincing evidence that brands that do best over time are brands that find a voice and stick to it. They don't throw things out every time some researcher comes up with a new way to 'improve' their marketing strategy or ad campaign. I guarantee you, if you hire a researcher she will 100% of the time find a way to 'improve' what you are doing - no matter how good it is. That's what they think they're getting paid for.

In 2016, some idiots at Heineken, the owners of Dos Equis beer, fired "The Most Interesting Man in the World." At the time, it was without question the most popular and successful campaign in its category and one of the best-loved campaigns of the first part of the century.

According to the marketing geniuses at Heineken the reason for firing TMIMITW (The Most Interesting Man in the World) was to 'contemporize' the campaign. You know there is a big fat powerpoint deck written by some cliché-spewing data monkey somewhere telling them that they had to 'contemporize' the campaign by 'engaging the millennial target' — just as every strategic document in the world today is required by law to say we have to 'engage the Gen-Z target.'

So they hired a newer, younger TMIMITW. It was a complete disaster.

Dos Equis identified a non-existent   problem and force-fed an unnecessary solution. A few months later they fired the agency. When incompetent marketers are at the wheel, agencies are always the roadkill.

The unquenchable thirst of bungling marketers to fuck with good things is among the most dangerous of habits. It comes from the ignorant belief that something new is always better.

Some marketers simply cannot leave good enough alone. If you ever hear a marketer or advertiser use the term 'wear-out' about a successful campaign, fire him on the spot. Great marketing and advertising ideas do not wear out. It's the discipline of incompetent marketers that wears out.

Advertising's First Responders

When I first published the essay called *The Three Word Brief*, I was not surprised to hear from marketing people who disagreed with me. The people I heard from generally made this case: Fame without a reason is empty and worthless. They said that positioning and differentiation are the first job of advertising strategy because they give substance to fame. In other words, positioning and differentiation are the factors that make fame productive.

This is wrong. In fact, it's exactly the opposite. Fame, inherently, creates the strongest type of positioning and differentiation. The most powerful *differentiator* for any brand is to be the most famous in its category. The most powerful *position* for any brand is to be the most famous in its category.

Differentiation and positioning have become primary elements of brand strategy. There's no doubt that these ideas have a certain logic and appeal to them. For many years I subscribed to them. They have allowed the marketing and branding industries to create a very believable and comfortable narrative for the past few decades about how brand strategy should be approached and what the key components of advertising strategy should be.

Today, however, I believe these ideas are secondary. I don't believe that consumers react very well to the logic of the marketing industry. I believe consumers react to brand associations and aesthetics — symbols, icons, images, slogans, melodies and other distinguishing artifacts. Ask people on the street how Coors is different from Budweiser; how Nike is different from Adidas; how Coke is different from Pepsi. I don't think you'll hear the language of brand briefs. I think you'll hear the language of logos, symbols, design, slogans, and melodies.

As stated earlier, I call these impressionistic attributes. Behavioral economics has demonstrated pretty convincingly that a lot of human behavior is driven by mental activities that we are not quite conscious of and are post-rationalized with logic. It would seem reasonable that brand preferences might also entail mental activities in which brand associations are the first responders and are subsequently rationalized with logic.

The Human Factor

Business people, like scientists, are used to thinking that there is a logical explanation for every phenomenon. We may not know the answer now, but given the right tools, the right methodology (you may substitute the right metrics and the right data) and enough time, we can find an explanation for all consumer behavior.

I'm not so sure. The idea that motivating people is simply about finding the right "answer" may ultimately result in our arriving at the same conclusion we have reached about the physical world -- it is way stranger and way more mystifying than we imagine.

Under certain circumstances, a brand can be described as having a powerful effect on a consumer and in certain circumstances the same brand may have little to no effect on the same consumer.

The same person may buy a brand whose advertising she likes, as well as brands whose advertising she hates.

The same person may buy products that are clearly differentiated and products that are generic.

The same person may buy products that are exceptionally good values, and some that are hideously overpriced.

This is not unusual. This duality is pretty typical of consumer behavior. There are inherently contradictory behaviors that confound us and mock our most cherished beliefs about consumer behavior. I'm going to invent an obnoxious term here, but it's necessary to communicate what I'm trying to say. The term is 'behavior plasticity.'

Behavior plasticity, or the inconsistency of consumer behavior, is a mysterious and confusing element of marketing. It is one factor that marketing people continuously misunderstand in their struggles to describe and predict consumer behavior. Believing in the orthodoxy of one marketing philosophy, one media philosophy, or one creative philosophy is a trap that disguises the mysterious and fascinating real-world behavior of consumers.

Human behavior can be described in ways that are contradictory, but equally true. Sometimes you feel like a nut, sometimes you don't.

Our Principle Problem

In most fields of endeavor progress is achieved by the accretion of knowledge over time.

In medicine, for example, we learned of the germ theory of disease. Then we learned that germs were spread by dirty things like flies, mosquitoes, and sex. But it all started with the basic knowledge that diseases weren't caused by frogs or witches, but by germs.

In aeronautics, the materials we use to make airplanes are completely different from the ones used one hundred years ago. But we still use the same fundamental design of a fuselage and a pair of wings. The principles of air travel are over one hundred years old (sadly, so is the food) but the principles are still being built on.

Copernicus taught us that the universe did not revolve around the Earth, but that the Earth revolved around the sun. Then we discovered that there were other bodies revolving around the sun. Then Newton figured out the mechanism for all this - gravity. One discovery leads to another.

Advertising is different. We respect no history. We observe no principles. We have no connective tissue. Every generation tosses out what was learned before and declares it dead. Every generation invents its own dreadful jargon that for a brief time passes for wisdom – engagement, conversations, storytelling, empowerment.

The absence of verifiable principles is the dirty little secret behind why we engender such timid respect in the business community.

In most disciplines there are unifying principles. Some examples: Physics has the law of conservation of energy. Biology has natural selection. Economics has supply and demand. These are fundamental to the nature of the endeavor. In advertising, what are the proven unifying fundamental principles that we all accept? If there are any, I don't know what they are. A field of endeavor without principles is not a discipline – it's a free for all.

What do we believe in now? Engagement, conversations, storytelling, and empowerment? These aren't principles. These are the dreadful clichés of a tired industry.

Philosophy or Donuts?

Several years ago a very sincere guy who ran a chain of donut shops came to see me. He wanted to do an advertising campaign.

"We're different," he explained. "We're a commune. Everyone who works here owns an equal part. We work cooperatively. It's a model for how businesses should be run. It's a vision of the future. I think we should do an ad campaign about it. I think people will really respond."

"How are your donuts?" I asked.

"They're very good." He said.

"Then forget the philosophy," I said. "Nobody needs more philosophy. They need good donuts."

Advertising Is a Weak Force

Gravity is everywhere. Consequently, we think of gravity as a powerful force that keeps us glued to the ground. Actually, science tells us that gravity is a very weak force. In fact, it is the weakest known force in the universe.

To prove this to yourself, go to a children's toy shop and buy one of those little horseshoe magnets. Then put a paper clip on the ground. Place the magnet near the paper clip. You now have two competing forces – the electro-magnetic force of a little magnet versus the gravitational force of the entire planet Earth. The little magnet wins.

Why? Because science tells us that the electro-magnetic force happens to be 1,000,000,000,000,000,000,000,000,000,000,000,000,000 times stronger than gravity.

Gravity is all around us. So we think of it as a strong force. Same with advertising. We are exposed to thousands of advertising messages every day. Only a tiny proportion of them make any impression on us at all. As a whole, advertising is a weak force. But like an airplane falling to earth, every now and then there is a big advertising success and the ad industry takes it as proof of the extraordinary power of ads. In fact, it is proof of only one thing — the extraordinary power of *great* ads.

In fact, there are only two ways in which big advertising successes usually occur — great creative work or large expenditures of money.

One way to be successful at advertising is to spend a lot of money. Some brands have stayed near the top of their categories for decades without ever having created a memorable ad. They remain successful in part due to the force of spending boatloads of money.

Obviously, doing outstanding ads is a far more desirable strategy. The problem is that doing great ads is way more difficult than it sounds. You've probably noticed that about 95% of all ads are crappy and derivative. And so are about the same percent of books, songs, and paintings. If you think all this crappy stuff exists because people aren't trying hard, you're wrong. The reason is actually quite simple: producing great stuff is really, really hard. And there are very few people who can do it. Nobody sets out to create a crappy ad or a crappy book or a crappy song. They just turn out that way.

Creative talent is a very rare and very precious commodity. Not everyone has it. As a matter of fact, hardly anyone has it. It takes a lot of talent to make a weak force strong.

Are Creative Ads More Effective?

As long as I've been in the advertising business there has been a very large question smoldering under the surface of my skin: Does advertising that we deem to be more creative actually produce better business results, or is that just a fond wish that 'creative people' and our supporters have invented to justify treating advertising as an art, and not just a blunt instrument?

As a former copywriter and creative director I am a strong believer in the power of creativity in advertising. In fact, every neuron in my tiny little brain is committed to that belief. But there is another part of my brain (the part that used to be a science teacher) that tries to remind me about intellectual honesty, and keeps saying to me, 'How do you know this?'

The studies that I have seen and read generally seem to take the following form. The researcher starts with a group of ads that have been recognized as exceptionally creative by experts or by respected awards organizations and compares their real-world business effectiveness to advertising that has not been recognized as such. The results are often convincing, and the 'creative' ads exhibit significantly superior effectiveness.

An argument one could make against this methodology (which I will not make) is that it is dependent on two factors that ought not be taken at face value. First, that the experts and award committees are actually able to accurately discern levels of creativity. Creativity is a notoriously difficult thing to define and the idea that the people who have been tasked with defining it are particularly qualified to do so is a difficult case to prove.

The second argument against this methodology is about the business results that are used to measure effectiveness. How do we know they are reliable? As someone who has written more than his share of case histories, I am very aware of the effect that imaginative writing can play in the description of success.

If the people assessing creativity are not uniquely qualified to do so, and if the measures of effectiveness are not wholly reliable, then the conclusions cannot be taken seriously.

But, as stated, I am not going to criticize the methodology on this basis. For the sake of argument, let's assume that the experts and awards committees are fully qualified to define and assess creativity and the metrics that are used to define business success are fully accurate.

I still have a problem.

Creative awards are usually presented in the year following the initiation of a campaign. You can't give awards for advertising created in any year until the year is over. Consequently, awards committees and experts usually don't get together to make their determinations until awards season, a few months into the following year.

So there can be a lag time of between 12 and 18 months between the time a campaign launches and the determination of its level of creativity by the experts. In this lag period there is every opportunity for the people who are going to be charged with defining creativity at a later date to be exposed to the business results of campaigns. Trade publications, advertising insiders, the business section of newspapers, and industry gossip are reporting on winners and losers every day of the year.

It is likely that the experts are reading and hearing reports of advertising successes and failures throughout the year. By the time they are tasked with determining levels of creativity, the experts and the awards committees have a very good idea of which campaigns produced highly effective advertising the previous year and which campaigns fell flat. Is it realistic to expect these people to ignore what they know about success and failure when they are assessing standards of creativity? I find that hard to believe.

It seems to me only natural that an individual will give higher grades for creativity to a campaign she knows to have been effective than to one she knows to have bombed. It seems highly unlikely that an awards judge will deem a campaign very creative if he knows the campaign was a disaster, the agency was fired, the marketing director replaced and the campaign pulled.

They also may have knowledge of the agencies or individuals who are responsible for the advertising and the creative reputations of these agencies or individuals. If this is the case, their evaluation of creativity may have been contaminated by cultural expectations or knowledge of, or inferences about, the the talent of the creators.

I am not implying that experts and awards committees are remiss in their duties or unprincipled in their decision making. I am merely suggesting that they are human. The likelihood that a human will take something he knows to have been a massive failure and compare it favorably to something he knows to have been a massive success is not high.

If this is the case the process can be, to a worrying degree, a tautology. Campaigns known to have been effective are presented as being highly creative, and campaigns deemed highly creative are presented as proof of superior effectiveness.

If we are to be rigorous in our assessment of creativity our methodology needs to adhere to the accepted standards for all other types of rigorous research. In which case the experts assigned to assessing creativity should be required to do so "blind." They should do so without knowing who created the advertising, any commentary on the advertising, any knowledge of the success or failure of the brand in question. This is the only way we can get a pure assessment of creativity without the unconscious contamination of outside influences or *a priori* inferences of success by the judges. In other words, we can probably never get a pure assessment of creativity.

I still firmly believe that creativity is the most important determination of advertising effectiveness. But I wish I had a more substantial, scientific basis for that belief.

***

After I first published the above piece, several people commented that the only criterion for creativity in advertising is sales success. If it sells, it's creative. If it don't, it ain't. I reject this out of hand. Without getting into a deep philosophical discussion, let me give three simple reasons why this is not acceptable.

First, I would point to the argument made by Byron Sharp in *"How Brands Grow"* that one of advertising's primary functions is not always to grow sales, but to maintain sales and market share and justify premium pricing. Or as he says, keep the airplane at 35,000 feet. In a highly competitive world, it can take an effective advertising effort just to keep many high-flying brands aloft. This is rarely taken into account in most analyses of ad effectiveness.

Second, I would argue that the long-term effect of advertising on brand success is very hard to tease out of sales results that are calculated on shorter time scales. Sales effectiveness over the course of time periods taken into account by awards shows is not necessarily indicative of long-term big picture effectiveness. I will once again defer to Prof. Sharp as well as Mark Ritson and Binet and Field who all make a compelling case for assessing the effectiveness of advertising over years.

Third, one of the things that makes advertising a fascinating subject (and a frustrating one to practitioners) is the role of probability. While I firmly believe that creativity in advertising is a massive advantage over banality, I also recognize that advertising I deem highly creative has an inconvenient record of failure. In advertising there are only likelihoods and probabilities. I think I can safely predict that when the day comes that I am satisfied I have seen a scientifically valid description of the relationship between creativity and effectiveness, creativity will be found to be not a guarantee of advertising success, just a more likely outcome.

Furthermore, and perhaps most important of all, if you assert that the only criterion for creativity is sales results, you are once again trapped in a tautology: Creative advertising is more effective because effective advertising is more creative.

Inevitably, there were the dreary semantic arguments. What do we mean by "creative?" What do we mean by "effective?" I don't want to go down that rabbit hole because there is no way out. Let me just assert (without an ounce of proof) that competent ad people know what we mean by creative and competent business people know what we mean by effective. Let's leave it at that.

Just as in any form of art or craft, creativity is often experienced subjectively. But that doesn't mean it has no objective reality. To define creativity strictly as a function of sales success is to reject creativity as an objective reality. To do so in advertising is no different from repudiating it in all forms of art, music, and literature. Advertising may not have the same goals or gravitas as art, music, or literature, but it can still be measured by the same standards of excellence. It also can be subject to the same pitfalls. Creativity without purpose can soon become indistinguishable from self- indulgence.

Maybe there exists a study I am not aware of that proves the case and would meet my standard of scientific rigor. In fact, I hope that somewhere there is. Until then I will be stuck in my personal predicament.

Do I believe creative advertising is really more effective than mundane advertising? Without question.

Can I prove it to you? Not exactly.

Tyranny of Strategy

Strategies are not written by God. They are written by planners, researchers, MBAs and other mildly boneheaded mortals.

Good creative people sometimes have a better feel for the problem than the committee that wrote the strategy. Sadly, they are often confronted with the brief only after the Committee of the Boneheaded have committed it to the inflexible logic of official documents.

If you're a decision maker, when you are evaluating a campaign idea that does not conform to the official brief, it's not enough to say 'this is off strategy'. You must also ask yourself, 'is this a better strategy than the one the committee came up with?'

If the answer is yes, you're going to have a lousy week. You have to go back and un-sell a strategy that has probably taken months to develop, has been up and down the organization, and has lots of (often questionable) data to back it up. Somehow, you have to convince a whole bunch of people that the work they've been doing for the past few months is wrong.

Sound impossible? That's why you get the big bucks.

Ego and Failure

In every enterprise requiring more that five human beings, a hierarchy will evolve. When the activity in question is advertising, the evolution of the hierarchy creates difficult situations. Client-agency relationships are not exempt from this law and if not handled properly the hierarchy can go a long way to undermining the best intentions of the group.

Here's how it should work.

At every client organization there is one person who is the real advertising decision maker. In some companies it's the CMO. In some companies it's the CEO. In some companies it's the brand manager. Their title is irrelevant. The real decision maker is the person who can say "yes, go do it" without having to ask permission.

At every ad agency, there is one person who is the account's real creative leader. On some accounts it's the exec creative director. On some accounts it's the art director. On some accounts it's the president of the agency. Their title is irrelevant. The real creative leader is the person that the real decision maker trusts and looks to for guidance.

The best creative work happens when the real decision maker and the real creative leader have a good relationship and work closely together. The worst creative work is always the result of layers of people supervising layers of people.

Working in a marketing department is tough. The hours are grueling. The work is tedious. The finance, operations, and sales people probably think you're a bozo. You're always having to justify your budget. But there is a little fun – you get to attend creative presentations.

Working in an account services or creative department at an agency is tough. The work is frustrating. The client always has you on the defensive. But there is a little fun – you get to attend creative presentations. Because marketing departments and agencies are difficult and frustrating places to work, and because agencies and clients want to keep their people happy, these people have been given an entitlement -- they can come to creative presentations.

Packing the room with client and agency people just makes the process tougher. But it's essentially impossible for an agency manager to tell an account director or a creative director, "I don't want you in the presentation." It's virtually impossible for a CMO to say to a brand manager, "You really don't need to be there." Egos simply can't tolerate this.

If you are an agency that wants to do good work on an account, someone in your creative department has to develop a good working relationship with the real decision maker on that business. If you are a client that wants good creative work, you've got to undo the entitlements, and let the real decision maker at your company work directly with the real creative leader on your account.

After 100 years in the agency business, I still have no idea how to create great ads. It's a code I haven't cracked. But I do know how to sell them. Get your real creative leader together with the real decision maker, and get everyone else out of the fucking way.

Let's Do It On The Floor

At one point in my career I was creative director for the US operation of an Australia- based agency called Mojo. Mojo was recognized as one of the world's really good creative shops. At one point while I was there it was named "International Advertising Agency of the Year" by Advertising Age. It was ultimately bought by Jay Chiat and re-christened Chiat/Day/ Mojo. During my tenure there I learned a very important lesson about presenting creative work from Alan (Mo) Morris and Allan (Jo) Johnston. Mo and Jo were unpretentious oddballs. They had a dread of big meetings, fancy presentations, and anything that smacked of formality. They shared an office and worked as a creative team, although they were both copywriters.

They sometimes used a very unusual and successful method of presentation. When they had an idea, they would call the real decision maker at the client company and invite him (usually a man in those days) over to the agency. It would be Mo, Jo and the Big Guy. No account people, no researchers, no brand babblers, no observers.

They would sit in their office and spread the layouts or storyboards on the floor, and then they'd explain the ideas. No big set-ups. No Powerpoint. No parsing every word of the brief. None of the tortured logic of account planning. None of the usual agency rituals that turn creative presentations into torment and agony.

It removed all the major obstacles to a successful presentation...

...the anxiety of 'the big show'

...playing to the crowd

...the irrelevant opinions of onlookers

Their technique was successful, and it helped them sell what they wanted to sell. It is without question a better way to accomplish the primary goal of both agency and client -- to produce better advertising. And yet, because of the structure and politics of most client organizations and most agency organizations, this method of operation is almost impossible.

Reality at the DMV

Last week I had the good fortune to spend an hour renewing my driver's license.

Most people would consider a trip to the DMV about as appealing as listening to a fifty-slide powerpoint about search engine optimization. But I'm thinking of making a monthly visit to the DMV a condition of employment for everyone on my staff.

I want them to see what the people they're making ads for really look like. I want them to see the people they never see at the restaurants they go to; never see at the bars they frequent; never see at the focus groups they attend; and never hear from on LinkedIn. In other words, I want them to see 'the consumer' they're all so very certain they know everything about.

As the CEO of a substantial European media company said in an email to me recently: *"There is a huge problem in America where the people making decisions, who grew up in comfortable homes, went to expensive colleges and landed relatively plush jobs, think that the Average American is just like them. It just isn't true but this mindset frames enormous decisions in many industries including media."*

So, please, do yourself a favor. Go to your nearest non-leafy DMV and spend an hour. And see if you come away still thinking that America is online having 'conversations about brands.'

,

You've Got a Brand Problem

There was a time when every problem seemed to be a 'communications' problem.

If you couldn't get along with your husband, you weren't 'communicating'. If your kid was incorrigible, you probably couldn't 'get through' to him. If your boss didn't like you, you weren't 'on the same wavelength.' There seemed to be no problems of substance, just problems of communication.

Well, the truth is, sometimes your husband is just a pain in the ass, and your kid is a nasty little shit, and your boss thinks you're worthless. And all the 'communication' in the world won't help. In fact, it will usually hurt.

Today we have the business version of this. Instead of communication, the catch-all problem in marketing today is 'the brand.' So if your products are crappy, or your stores are dirty, or your service is lousy, or your business strategy is stupid, you, my friend, have a brand problem. Call in the branding consultants!

Pay them a few hundred thou and let them study your brand for a few months. You see, solving real problems requires unpleasantness. Systems have to be changed. Products have to be redesigned. Idiots have to be fired. Floors have to be swept and walls have to be painted.

Brand tinkering, on the other hand, is generally quite agreeable. All it requires is money and a bunch of congenial meetings. Hire some branding consultants. Appoint a task force. Interview "stakeholders". Conduct focus groups. Have an off-site or two at a nice hotel. Change the logo. Define your 'brand purpose.' Tinkering with the brand is so much more pleasant than fixing the problems.

Unfortunately, after the money has been spent and the navel-gazing brand babblers have gone home, someone still has to sweep the floor, paint the walls, change the systems, and fire the idiots.

The Most Powerful Force In Marketing

Think of all the amazing new things that have been introduced in the past few years. In the digital realm alone, there have been thousands of astounding new products and services.

Every day I stumble on new offerings on the web that I had no idea existed that amaze me with their utility and creativity. The startling fact, however, is how few of them become successful businesses. According to the U.S. Bureau of Labor Statistics only 25% of new businesses achieve long-term success. Some published reports put the success rate of tech companies substantially lower.

The reason so many new products and new ideas do not succeed is a function of human psychology -- the reluctance of people to do something different.

Most companies either don't understand this or choose to ignore it. Marketers always overestimate the attractiveness of new things and underestimate the power of traditional consumer behavior.

I have been involved in the development of many new products and a lot of advertising campaigns for new products. Almost every new product I've been associated with has been either a reasonably good idea or an improvement on what went before. But most weren't compelling enough to overcome consumer attachment to doing what they usually do.

One of the biggest mistakes a marketer can make is taking too seriously what people say about a product in the development stage. When consumers are exposed to it, they will tell you it's a good idea. But what they can never tell you is whether it's a good *enough* idea to overcome the pull of their ongoing habits.

The most powerful force in marketing is not price, quality, distribution, advertising, or branding -- it's inertia.

Storytelling or Personalization. Pick One

For the past couple of years, the advertising industry has been fixated on two themes. The creative side of the business has been preoccupied with "storytelling," and the media side has been hooked on "personalization."

What no one seems to realize is that these two goals are contradictory. We'll get to that in a minute. First, a little overview.

The dumbest idea of advertising's digital age has been "interactivity." Consumers who could barely stand to *watch* or *read* ads anymore were suddenly going to want to *interact* with them and join *conversations* about them.

Because people wanted to interact with pop musicians, famous athletes, and movies stars we thought they'd want to interact with us. Not. The idea that the same consumer who was gleefully clicking her remote to escape from TV ads was going to joyfully click her mouse to interact with online ads is going to go down as one of the great marketing fantasies of all time.

Our second dumbest idea is "personalization." Somewhere marketers got the idea that personalized one-to-one targeting is superior to mass media reach.

Amazingly, the same people who babble on about "personalization" also won't shut up about "storytelling." They can't see the contradiction. They don't understand that storytelling and personalization are enemies. Storytelling is about shared, universal narratives. Personalization is about individualized messages.

Jesus on the cross, Joan of Arc at the stake, George Washington and the cherry tree are not "personalized." They are powerful storytelling because they are universal. They are known by masses of people. That's their power.

If you want to create successful stories you have to tell them out loud and in public. If you want to get all personal you have to do it privately.

We have become so absorbed in our own insular feedback loop that we have lost any sense of the connection marketing has to the basics of human communication. You can't be pro-storytelling and anti-mass media.

As usual the marketing industry is so far up its own ass with its new technology toys that technology trumps common sense. The fact that we *can* do personalized, one-to-one advertising is not a compelling reason why we *should*.

The Handsomest Man in the World

That's me. The handsomest.

What? You don't believe me? I have affidavits from my mother, my wife, and several of my employees. I have awards from the American Association of Old Fat Bald Guys.

What? You still don't believe? You think I'm lying?

Okay, maybe I'm not really the handsomest. Maybe I'm just trying to make a point. The point is this. You would think that one of the first things people trained in advertising would learn is that what you *say* can be very different from what you *communicate*. I can walk into a room and say, "I am the handsomest man in the world." What I am communicating, however, is "I am a great big jerk."

Not one person in the room will believe that I am the handsomest man in the world, and everyone in the room will believe I am a jerk.

When you say something that no one believes, you are not only wasting your money, you are undermining your credibility. And all the spurious support points in the world don't make absurd claims any more believable. Yet advertisers continue to ignore the distinction between what they are saying and what they are communicating.

Electronics retailers continue to talk about their great customer service. Banks continue to talk about the importance of relationships. Computer peripheral manufacturers continue to talk about plug and play. All they are communicating is that they are bullshit artists who can't be trusted.

Sidewalk Psychologists

Once upon a time, advertising people decided that they no longer wanted to talk about their products. Instead they decided it would be more productive to be amateur psychologists. So instead of making ads about the attributes of their products, they started making ads about the imagined psychological profiles of their customers.

I was reading an article in USA Today about a new ad campaign for a large company whose name I'm not going to tell you yet. The reason I'm not going to tell you is that I want you to look at their strategy and tell me if you can figure out who these people are and what they are selling. Or even what category they are competing in.

The corporation in question had this to say about their media strategy:

"...we focus on a target audience based on a psychographic profile. Our target is the everyday hero and they share five core values: family first, work-life balance, self knowledge and fulfillment,

spirit of independence, and fun and enjoyment. The other thing we know about (them) is they take great pride in staying true to themselves.."

I've seen similar bullshit in about a thousand planning briefs. So here's what I want to know. Who are they *not* targeting? Who *doesn't*...

...put family first

...want work-life balance

...seek self-knowledge and fulfillment

...have a spirit of independence

...seek fun and enjoyment.

...take great pride in staying true to themselves

If they 'focus on a target audience', who exactly is *not* in their target audience?

And now the big reveal: Who do you think this company is and what are they selling? Cars? Lipstick? Golf clubs? Running shoes? Cruises? Clothing? Beer? Vitamin water? Organic chicken? Life insurance? Underwear?

The company is Holiday Inn.

Here's some free advice for them. I've been to a Holiday Inn recently. I didn't see too many people wandering around looking for 'self-knowledge and fulfillment.' Mostly they were looking for clean towels and a bucket of ice.

Road to Reality

Marketing's reality erosion began over ten years ago. We were treated to a glorious vision of the future. The ensuing decade was expected to be one of the most fruitful and productive in the history of marketing. We had amazing new tools and amazing new media that we never had before.

- Our ability to personalize advertising and reach consumers 'one-to- one' was sure to make advertising more relevant, more timely, and more likable.

- Our ability to listen to consumer conversations through social media and react quickly couldn't help but connect brands more closely with their customers.

- The opportunity for people to interact with media was certain to make advertising and marketing more engaging.

And yet, by the near unanimous opinion of marketing professionals, marketing has gotten less effective, not more. Advertising has gotten worse, not better. Rather than creating communication that is more relevant, more timely and more likable we are creating communication that is more annoying, more disliked, and more avoided.

A headline in *The New York Times* asserted, "The Advertising Industry Has A Problem. People Hate Ads." Research indicates that regard for our industry is at a new low. It's gotten so bad we have half the trustworthiness of lawyers.

But don't believe me. Let's do an experiment. Let's use *you* as a test of the depth of marketers' reality disintegration. Let's have a look at your behavior and see how it correlates with the practices and beliefs of our industry.

I want you to start by thinking about your refrigerator. Think about all the stuff that's in there: The cheese, the juices, the jelly, the butter, the beer, the soda, the mayonnaise, the bacon, the mustard...

Now think about your pantries. The cereals, the beans, the napkins, the flour, the detergent, the sugar, the rice, the bleach, the paper towels...

Next your bathroom cabinet. The toothpaste, the pain relievers, the shampoo, the soap, the bandages, the deodorant, the cosmetics...

Now your closet and dresser. Your socks, your underwear, your shirts, your pajamas, your swim suit, your t-shirts, your sweaters, your pants...

Now your car. The battery, the tires, the wiper blades, motor oil, gasoline, the air filter, the muffler...

Now answer these questions:

- Do you 'share branded content' about any of this stuff?
- Do you feel 'personally engaged' with these brands?
- Do you 'join the conversation' about any of this stuff?

- Do you 'co-create' with any of these brands?

- Do you feel like you are part of these products 'tribes' or 'communities?'

If you don't, why in the world do you believe anyone else does? Because some marketing big shots said so? Because your boss says so? Because all the people around you say so? All this questionable brand involvement ideology is the delusional framework on which a great deal of marketing activity is currently constructed.

The real world is a harsh and unwelcoming place for marketers. In the real world, consumers are massively not joining conversations about our brands. Despite the incessant babbling of brand strategists, consumers are overwhelmingly not committed to having relationships with our brands. They do not want to engage with our content, and are not fascinated by our brand stories. They do not consider themselves part of a community or tribe that has our brand at the center.

The ideas we have about our customers' involvement with our brands are largely fairy tales. And yet they are the bedrock upon which we have built an entire ideology of marketing communication.

The sad truth is, our relationship with the consuming public consists of a great many realities we have to cope with, and very few we can control. But our marketing activities do not account for this. We spend 100% of our marketing energy and dollars on the largely ineffectual exercise of trying to control consumer behavior, and 0% of our resources trying to cope with the realities of consumer behavior.

Everything that marketing communication people are doing should be analyzed through a hard-nosed assessment of real world consumer behavior, not the rosy lens of traditional brand and marketing thinking. How do marketing practices need to evolve if we accept that for the most part consumer relationships with brands are more transactional than emotional?

Formulating our marketing and advertising activities from a real world perspective may lead to startling insights and revolutionary strategies. Or it may convince us that our current efforts are on the right track. Most likely, it will lead to a little of each.

Public Advertising vs Private Advertising

Among the obsessions of the digital age of advertising has been the drive for personalization. It is taken for granted that the more personalized an ad is and the more precisely it is targeted, the more effective it is likely to be. There are very few in our industry who question this assumption. And yet, it is highly questionable.

I would like to suggest that the main power of advertising is not in precision targeting, it is in mass targeting. The real power in advertising is in having large numbers of people familiar with and comfortable with your brand. A realistic view of the world's most successful brands gives us a very clear and unambiguous picture — spreading the word is far more likely to create success than concentrating it. In 2024, the CEO of Nike learned this lesson the hard way.

In the long run, getting a lot of people familiar with your brand and comfortable with it has a much higher probability of building your business than any other theory of advertising communication. Most marketers are famously inept at creating a consequential differentiation for their brand. That's why god created advertising. A poorly differentiated brand everybody's heard of has a lot better chance of success than a well-differentiated brand that nobody's heard of.

The proponents of personalized one-to-one advertising tell us that one-to-one targeted advertising is more capable of performing successfully than mass targeting. Really? Do they think Donald Trump would have become president of the US if *The Apprentice* had been a webinar?

There are several cogent arguments for not accepting the idea that personalization and precision targeting are superior to generalized strategy and mass reach. In arguing against personalization, I'm going to radically summarize (I hope without misrepresenting) a few ideas on the subject proposed by people other than and smarter than myself.

Rory Sutherland, Vice Chairman of Ogilvy, UK points out that fame imparts singular benefits on people and companies. At the most basic level, people are more likely to choose famous products over unknown products. Let's do a little thought experiment.

You've been driving all morning on a two-lane highway and you're getting hungry. You come to the small town of Nowheresville and at the intersection there are two hamburger joints. One is McDonald's, the other is Bubba's Burgers.

It is likely that Bubba makes a better burger than McDonald's. But it is also more likely that you will choose McDonald's. Why? I think the answer goes something like this: While you might like to have a better burger, it's more important that you don't have a *terrible* burger. While you might like to stop at a place that is comfortable and relaxing, it's more important that you don't stop at a place that *is gross* and has six months of dried snot stuck to the bottom of the table.

McDonald's may not make a great burger, and it may not be the most elegant environment, but you have a reasonable expectation that the burger won't make you sick and the tables have been cleaned. In other words, Bubba's may very well make a better burger, but McDonald's is good enough, and relatively risk free. The aversion to risk trumps the possibility of incremental superiority.

So the question is, why do you believe McDonald's is good enough and safer? I think the answer is simple. McDonald's is famous. The underlying logic is that famous brands *can't afford* to be too dangerous or gross.

Another way of understanding the value of fame is called signaling. In a paper in the Journal of Advertising Research, December 2004, by Tim Ambler and E. Ann Hollier entitled, *"The Waste In Advertising Is The Part That Works"* Ambler and Hollier describe the value of signaling.

In the previous section, "The Handsomest Man in the World," I have described how you may say one thing but signal another. The argument that Ambler and Hollier make is that mass targeted advertising is also a form of signaling. Regardless of the message, it tells the world that you are a substantial company, that you have deep resources that are underpinned by success, and that you believe in your product enough to spend large sums of money to support it. As Doc Searls describes it, *"it is akin to a male peacock's fanned-out tail. It speaks of the company's substance, and the fact that it can afford to advertise."* And do it widely.

A third reason to question personalized advertising is described as 'cultural imprinting.' This is a term invented by Kevin Simler. The logic supporting his cultural imprinting idea is that in some way we all want to be part of what is culturally acceptable.

As he says, brand images are *"part of the cultural landscape we inhabit. They provide cultural information. When we ignore brand messages we're missing out on valuable cultural information and alienating ourselves from the Zeitgeist."* He says this puts us in danger of becoming outdated, unfashionable, or otherwise socially hapless. We become like *"the kid who wears his dad's suit to his first middle school dance."* In other words, in some way brand choices send messages to others about who we are. And no one but a sociopath wants to send the wrong message.

So what does all this have to do with the personalization problem? In Simler's words *"cultural imprinting relies on the principle of common knowledge. For a fact to be common knowledge among the group, it's not enough for everyone to know it. Everyone must also know that everyone else knows it."* In other words, part of our purchasing calculation is not just our belief that Z is an acceptable product, but our expectation that other people believe Z is acceptable because they know what we know.

In mass media, I know what my friends are seeing. I know that if they're watching football they're seeing the same ads I am. Consequently I have reasonable confidence that my friends believe that Ford makes acceptable pick-up trucks and Budweiser makes beer I don't have to feel weird about.

But I have no idea what my friends are seeing online. If we all live in our own little personalized, one-to-one digi-world, I have no frame of reference for cultural imprinting. I don't know if my friends will think me an idiot for buying those headphones I saw advertised on *somewhereverycheap.com.*

In a nutshell, this may very well be why thus far mass-market advertising is demonstrably more effective at brand building than highly personalized advertising. Highly individualized, personalized advertising makes advertising a more private, rather than public experience. It creates uncertainty as to what advertising our friends are seeing. Which in some way keeps us from knowing what brands may be culturally acceptable.

To a significant degree, mass media is public advertising, and personalized one-to-one advertising is private advertising. If you're a brand marketer and you want to grow, you have two choices. Be 'wasteful' or be invisible.

What if Precision Targeting Doesn't Work?

What if most of the media targeting we do is unnecessary complexity masquerading as discipline? What if there are only one or two important pieces of data we need when planning media?

There is actually some science to back-up my heresy. According to research conducted by a professor at MIT, a fellow at the Melbourne Business School, and the Head of Operations and Technology at Group M, data that is informing your programmatic ad buys may not just be unproductive, it may be counterproductive. In one test, data bought from a data broker was able to correctly intuit the sex of an individual 43% of the time. If my cat flipped a coin she would be right 50% of the time.

A second test of data acquired from data brokers improved targeting performance by 184%. Sounds good right? The only problem is that acquiring that data... *"creates extra costs of about 238% on average in comparison to random placements."*

What if the only really important thing we need to know when planning media is whether a person participates in our category? What if the cost of further targeting exceeds the benefits it provides? If we're selling golf balls, the only important targeting question we have to ask is, 'Does this person play golf?' If we're selling wine the only important question to ask is, 'Does she drink wine?' If we sell tires the only important question is, 'Do they own a car?'

All the other stuff – their education, their income, their weight, height, and serial number, their zip code and psychosexual predilections, the websites they visited yesterday, and the number of chickens in their backyard – may be interesting, but what if they don't do a damn thing to make our media buys more effective or efficient?

During my semi-brilliant advertising career I would never have suggested such a thing to a client. Clients don't like oddball ideas. They are resolutely devoted to 'best practices' — ya know, believing what everybody else believes. And everyone else believes that leveraging data to create precision targeting is the future of advertising.

I'd love to see an advertiser do a split run. In one market buy media based on precision demographics, psychographics, data-o-graphics, graph-o-graphics, and bullshit-o-graphics.

In another matched market run the same campaign but make the media buy based on just one behavioral criterion – does the person participate in our category?

I'd love to see the cost-benefit results.

Advertising's Untold Stories

Have you ever wondered why the highly touted marketing miracles you read about in the press never seem to work for you?

Most of the information we get about the success or failure of advertising and marketing initiatives comes in the form of a story: a press release; an article in a trade publication; a feature in a news outlet or an online business report; a case history presented at an industry conference.

The stories that reach us are often superficial – they are mostly headlines lightly dusted with a few specifics, some meticulously curated numbers, and a generous helping of spin. This is because marketing strategies are valuable trade secrets and keeping them confidential can be important to business success. You don't just give 'em away. As a result, the narratives we get are often devoid of some important specifics that are key to understanding the true nature of the story.

Nonetheless, for every story to which we are exposed, there are a thousand untold stories we don't get to read or hear about. These are the non-spectacular stories, created in non-spectacular fashion, by non-spectacular brands. In other words, they are about 99% of everything that ever happens in marketing.

I don't think it's terribly controversial to suggest that we are far more likely to read success stories than failure stories. Ask any business reporter. The number of PR releases she gets about a brilliant new campaign being launched will outnumber the releases she gets about a dismal failure by about a zillion to one. After all, who wants to alarm the board, embarrass the CEO, scare the shareholders, and frighten the puppy dogs by revealing what bewildered bumblers they are? It's a lot wiser to be forthcoming about your successes and circumspect about your failures.

When this becomes terribly dangerous is not when it is applied to a specific case history, but when it is applied to primary information we get about marketing fundamentals.

I would wager great stacks of money that the untold stories of the mediocre performance of most marketing activities outnumber the widely circulated stories of success by a mile. This is doubly true of (but not limited to) whatever new marketing miracle happens to be trending this week.

The narratives we are exposed to about these marketing activities, and the belief we have in their efficacy are profoundly skewed by the bias toward trumpeting success and muting failure. This is perilous. It leads to conferences, books, and god help us, webinars extolling the effectiveness of marketing activities based on wildly unrepresentative samples. It gives our entire industry a false impression of the value of these undertakings. It leads us to throw money at expensive, wasteful tactics. And it reinforces the lemming-like attraction of naive marketers to the trendy fantasies that have dominated our industry for the past decade.

It is not that the stories themselves aren't true. It is that the results being reported may be wildly divergent from the results to be found in the total number of outcomes, the vast majority of which go unreported.

Before you take any report about an advertising or marketing tactic as indicative of a general truth, you'd be wise to assume that just the fact that it is being told at all makes it likely that it is one or two standard deviations from normal. You should assume that the overwhelming number of stories that haven't been told on the subject are not nearly as rosy.

In marketing, the untold stories are usually the real story.

Prisoners of Youth

After World War II something new arrived in the U.S. – the teenager. Previously, in all of history, there was no such thing. For centuries there were just young people who went out in the fields or down in the mines or over to the factories and worked their asses off. Overwhelmingly, the fruits of their labors and the imperatives of their lives were focused on the relentless struggle to keep themselves and their families alive. It was most often a brutally hard existence.

That changed over time. By the 1950's and 60's, unprecedented prosperity and affluence arrived and the teenager was born. A teenager was a young person who had what no other young person in history ever had – money and time.

With the teenager came something else that was completely new – youth culture. At first it was just music and language. But then a whole set of customs and values evolved including fashion, celebrities, attitudes, economics and imagery.

Coincidental with the rise of pop culture was the rise of the 'creative revolution' in advertising. In the beginning, advertising didn't have much use for pop culture. Have a look at the great ads from the early period of the 'creative revolution' (VW, Alka-Seltzer, etc.) and you'll see the ads were about products not lifestyles. The actors were grown-ups, and youth iconography didn't exist.

Slowly but surely youth culture worked its way into the advertising lexicon. At first it was thrilling. Young people were tickled to hear their favorite types of music and see people like them in ads. What made it exciting was that it was new and different.

Fifty years later, advertising has become tethered to youth culture in a way that is undermining imaginative thinking, harming our creative output, and seriously limiting marketing effectiveness. Youth culture and fashion have always been stupid. If you want to die an imbecile, don't pay attention to art, literature, history, science, or nature. Pay attention to Kardashians.

What has changed is that pop iconography is no longer the exception in advertising, it is now by far the dominant tool in the tool box. Pop culture is no stupider today than it was 50 years ago, it is just more pervasive. And that's a problem. As wealth and economic power have been hugely concentrated in the hands of mature people, youth culture rarely interests or engages the people who have and spend most of the money. In fact, it is often off-putting. But it has become the default language of advertising despite the fact that it is not the language of the people who drive our economy or dominate our commerce.

Worse, it is self-perpetuating. The more that marketing people see youth-orientation dominate advertising the more they unconsciously assume that it is the proper voice for advertising and that they better employ it, too. As a result, much of advertising has become a tiresome, one-note exercise in celebrity/music/technology banality. It creates a false feedback signal to marketers and the business community that pop culture/youth sensibility is the correct vocabulary for marketing.

There is nothing wrong with the use of celebrities or cultural trends in advertising so long as they are not used as shallow substitutes for ideas. Once a small percent of advertising leaned on pop culture as a replacement for creativity. Today that tactic is much more prevalent. The constant drum beat of music/celebrities/technology is everywhere and the wonderful surprise of unexpected, off-the-wall, illogical advertising is largely missing in action.

We are tethered to youth culture in a way that is harmful to our goals and to business. The attribute most noticeable in creative work is not imaginative thinking, it's the slavish conformity to whatever's trending. As usual, our obsessions have undermined our best interests.

One of the pernicious side-effects of this is our inability and, in fact, our blind refusal to speak to the people who have and spend most of the money in our economy. As a research paper from the UK said about our industry *"...we, like everyone else, prefer to talk to people we are familiar with and understand. Witness the industry's continued fixation with targeting 18-34... which is surely driven more by the composition of our industry than the demographic reality of our aging population and the massive concentration of wealth and spending."*

There are two reasons advertising agencies default to youth imagery. First, the people in agencies are overwhelmingly young and don't have the cultural vocabulary to speak comfortably to mature people. Look in any coffee shop and try to find someone in his 20's talking to someone in her 50's. I mean, other than saying, "Can I take your order?" When the people writing the ads are disconnected from the people buying the products, there is a problem. And while only six percent of agency employees are over fifty, fifty-seven percent of new car buyers are over fifty.

Second, binding to youth culture is such an easy and attractive way to seem relevant. Particularly if you have been seduced by advertising's feedback loop and don't understand the limited role young people actually play in our economy.

There is a lazy, unimaginative way to do advertising, and a difficult, inspired way. The lazy way has been the same for decades – find a pop song or celebrity and borrow some glow. The difficult, inspired way is to untether yourself from the banality of trendiness and search for something interesting to say.

Advertising Is Like Exercise

Here's what the ROI guys don't understand about advertising. They think you can advertise today and measure the results tomorrow. It doesn't work like that.

If you're not used to running, and you run five miles today, you will not be stronger or healthier or feel better tomorrow. As a matter of fact, you'll probably feel like crap. But if you run 5 miles every day, next year at this time you probably will be stronger, healthier, and feel better.

That's also how brand advertising works. If you advertise today, your business is not going to suddenly be successful tomorrow or next week. But if you advertise every day, over the next few years your business probably will get better, and healthier, and stronger.

Why do you think a can of Coca-Cola is worth 25¢ more than a can of Safeway cola? It's not because of the Coke ad you saw last night or last week. It's the ones you've seen your entire life.

Notice I said probably. There are no guarantees. Just like exercise, sometimes advertising backfires. You can take off on a five-mile run and have a heart attack after ten minutes. Or you could run all year and wind up with a gimpy knee. You never know. Similarly, you could advertise for a year and end up with nothing but a one-way ticket to bankruptcy court. You never know. It's all about likelihoods and probabilities.

If you look at the leading brands in mainstream categories, the likelihood is that they have one thing in common -- they advertise, and they do a lot of it. Does this mean that advertising is a surefire road to success? No. But absence of it is a pretty reliable road to failure.

Beware of Marketers with Ideologies

In 1996, best-selling author Seth Godin had this to say to Fast Company... *"I guarantee you that by the year 2000, Internet banner ads will be gone."* Oops.

Let's be fair to Seth. He's a smart guy and he has been right about a lot of things. But the problem with the above statement, like so many aspects of marketing these days, is that it is rooted in ideology. Seth's ideology was 'permission marketing.' He believed that the 'interruption model' of traditional advertising was on the way out, and that in order to communicate effectively with consumers, marketers would need their permission.

Like much of new age marketing philosophy, it sounded lovely. The problem is that the world isn't lovely. Having operating principles is fine, but being ideologically committed to a big idea often ends in a train wreck.

Ideology can be the downfall of pundits, historians and marketers. Philip Tetlock is an author and professor at the University of California-Berkeley. He's the winner of lots of impressive awards —

and an expert on experts. According to Tetlock, experts who are most often wrong are those who have an ideological commitment to a big idea. *"They tended to have one big, beautiful idea that they loved to stretch, sometimes to the breaking point. They tended to be articulate and very persuasive as to why their idea explained everything. The media often love (them.)"*

People attached to ideologies often are not able to adapt their big, beautiful idea to the constant surprises of the real world. Instead, they re-interpret the real world to fit their big, beautiful idea. In fact, what has happened is that contrary to permission model theory, the interruption model has become infuriatingly pervasive on the web. Every news, entertainment, and social media site is packed with ads that drive us all crazy. Meanwhile, permission marketing mainly allows us to preach to the converted. It may be beneficial for popular, high interest products and categories. But for the average business - a maker of vacuum cleaner bags or pencils or mufflers - it offers little in the way of leverage.

In the article quoted above, Godin also went on to say... *"Marketing is a contest for people's attention."* He is certainly right about that. However, the grand visions and big, beautiful new ideas about marketing that were supposed to help us gain people's attention in new ways have proven disappointingly hollow.

The result is that banner advertising — that horrible, corrupt, and maligned old thing — not only is not gone, it is metastasizing. We now call it display advertising and most of us wish it had disappeared in 2000 as Seth promised.

One of the lessons about marketing is that practicality consistently outperforms ideology.

Monty Python and Associates

It is my opinion that if they had chosen to, Monty Python would have been the best advertising agency in history. Why? Because they were very silly. One of the most underutilized and unappreciated tools in the advertising tool box is silliness.

Of course, MBAs and CMOs would strongly disagree with me. They believe in seriousness of purpose. They believe that the foundation for advertising effectiveness is built on a bedrock of strategic relevance. Monty Python would have taken these guys and slapped them with a fish.

While marketers take themselves and their jobs very seriously, most people see the advertising industry as both pompous and ridiculous. I believe they appreciate advertisers who don't take themselves seriously.

Effective advertising does not have to be relevant, or differentiating, or insightful or any of the other clichés we throw at it.

Its most propitious effect is to engage our 'enjoyment button.' Advertising that we enjoy is far more likely to be effective than advertising that preaches or shrieks at us.

Are relevance and differentiation and insight worthy goals? Sure. But engaging the impressionistic 'enjoyment button' is far more likely to be an effective tactic than a typical we're-better-than-them strategic ad proposition or a surprise-birthday-party-at-the-old-folks-home emotional cliché.

Advertising that tickles our humanity by being funny, beautiful, interesting, or entertaining has a much greater chance of being remembered and filed in our 'familiar and comfortable' mental file where, unbeknownst to us, most of our buying decisions are handled.

But, as with all endeavors of the imagination, silliness has its pitfalls. There are two kinds of silliness: silly-and-funny, and silly-and-stupid. There is nothing *less* funny than silly-and- stupid.

In order for silliness to be a valuable advertising asset, it must be funny. And that's where talent comes in. Silliness in the pursuit of laughs is a difficult needle to thread. There have been a thousand wannabe Monty Pythons who were very silly but just weren't funny enough. Imagination is present in all of us, but talent isn't.

If you want to engage an underutilized but highly effective advertising tactic, don't be afraid to be silly. But don't bother if you can't be funny.

Great Advertising Is the Best Strategy

People who are good at tennis tend to believe tennis is the greatest game. People who are good at painting tend to believe art is our highest calling. People who are religious believe in the brilliance of the bible. This is called confirmation bias. We tend to embrace those things that validate our beliefs or inclinations.

Advertising has two primary branches of discipline -- the strategic and the creative. The strategic part of advertising deals in logic and analysis. The creative part is concerned with imagination.

Most of us who work in advertising, perhaps 90% or more, are primarily involved in the strategic part. Although most of us don't have the word 'strategy' in our title, strategy is what we do. We decide how to spend media dollars, how to develop a promotion, how to present something to a committee, etc. In other words, we make strategic decisions. Is there a creative component to these strategic tasks? Sure. But in advertising the word 'creative' has a specific meaning. It relates to the development of advertising materials -- ads, designs, videos, etc, meant for dissemination to consumers. Most of us don't do that.

Our involvement with creative work is generally second-hand. We manage, evaluate or otherwise interact with it. But most of us are not involved in the hands-on making of it.

The consequence of this is that although it should be self-evident that the most important aspect of advertising is the advertising itself, our behavior says that we don't really believe this. We give great lip-service to creativity, but actually place a higher value on strategic tasks. Clients and agencies will allow themselves months to develop strategies, and days to create ads. We have endless hours of meetings, presentations, off-sites, deep-dives, decks, and downloads to discuss strategy. And at the end of all this, every now and then an ad appears.

Why? Because placing a higher value on strategy validates what we do. It is another example of confirmation bias.

This would be worth it if we could demonstrate that all this activity paid out. But the contribution of most people we blithely call 'strategists' to the effectiveness of advertising is suspect at best. It has been my experience that what passes for strategic insight in advertising is often quite unexceptional. It is usually some variation of *a)* quality and value, *b)* we're so hip, *c)* new and improved, *d)* we're authentic/ fresh/natural, or just some other clever way of saying something very mundane.

In fact, a typical brand's advertising strategy usually looks very much like its closest competitor's and provides very little in the way of leverage. Because of this, as Dave Trott brilliantly put it, many ad agencies have become 'the gift-wrapping department.' We take something ordinary and make it look nice.

Sadly, creative people these days cannot rely on anything very useful coming out of the briefs they get. When advertising breakthroughs occur, they are usually the result of an imaginative creative idea. This sometimes is the result of a well-thought out strategy, but very often comes from a creative person who understands the problem better than the strategy does.

A common reason for this is that as brands become bigger and more globalized, they become too big for specificity. They have to appeal to too many types of people in too many types of environments which leads to fluffy strategies that result in gift-wrapping instead of single-minded blueprints.

The homogenization of strategies is why imaginative thinking (creativity) has become so much more important, and so much harder to come by. Nonetheless, confirmation bias still leads the agency/client community to foolishly value the word of the most mediocre strategist above the instincts of the most talented creative person.

All this is just a long way of saying that, in most cases, great advertising is the best strategy.

And One More Thing

I've come a long way to discover something I think I've always known. Great advertising is great for all the wrong reasons.

It's not great because it differentiates your brand, or delivers a benefit, or has a call to action. Those are the things that *average* advertising does. And sadly, average advertising is pretty shitty.

Great advertising is different. It doesn't appeal to us as consumers, it appeals to us as humans. It is great because of an indefinable quality that leaves a singular impression. I have stolen the term "impressionism" to describe this phenomenon, but you can call it whatever you like.

The very best advertising is not about benefits or features; it's not about mysterious subconscious needs that can only be aroused emotionally. It's about talented people stimulating the fundamentals of our humanity.

Bob Hoffman

Part Two

INSIDE THE BLACK BOX

Utopia

There was a time, not that long ago, when many people believed in a kind of digital utopia.

My favorite quote from that period belongs to Arianna Huffington. She said, *"Thanks to YouTube -- and blogging and instant fact-checking and viral emails -- it is getting harder and harder to get away with repeating brazen lies without paying a price..."*

If only.

Among the fantasies that swirled around us at the time was an idea among marketing people that online advertising would provide us with almost perfect information about the efficacy of our endeavors. We would know exactly who we were reaching, what it cost us, and how the ad performed. This fantasy still lives among some in marketing.

Unfortunately, the real world has intruded on our fantasy world. In fact, there has never been a time when there has been more confusion, corruption, and misinformation about advertising. There has never been a time when advertisers chased rainbows, believed charlatans, and were taken to the cleaners by con men as they are now. And most of it is centered on online advertising - the very thing that was going to set us free.

About 80% of online advertising is bought "programmatically" *i.e.*, by computer programs. In a majority of cases, the buyers don't know...

...what they are buying

...who they are buying it from

...what they are getting

...what they are paying.

Nonetheless, marketers keep pouring in more and more money. This section will explore how advertisers are being cheated; why many advertisers don't know they're being cheated; why marketers who do know they're being cheated are afraid to acknowledge it; how advertising industry leaders have failed in their responsibilities; how perverse incentives compel marketers to keep the con alive; and what you can do to protect yourself.

Understanding the Black Box

In order to comprehend the black box of programmatic advertising we need to have at least a rudimentary picture of how it works.

There are essentially two ways to buy online advertising - directly and programmatically. When you buy directly, you go to a website owner (publisher) and make a deal with them.

When you buy programmatically you go to an ad exchange, hand over some money and some guidelines. The guidelines include a type of person you're trying to reach and an amount you're willing to pay. The exchange scans the web looking for your target consumer. When it finds a person who meets your criteria at a website, they bid on an ad slot on that website. If your bid wins, your ad appears on the website in front of that consumer. This all takes about a quarter of a second.

In the simplest possible terms, programmatic buying looks like this:

We start with an advertiser or agency.

The advertiser uses a DSP (Display Side Platform) which is software that helps automate the buying process.

The ad exchange is software that allows advertisers and publishers to buy and sell from a variety of ad networks.

The SSP (Supply Side Platform) is software that helps automate the selling of advertising

As we will soon see, in actuality the system is about a thousand times more complex than this diagram indicates and the ability of the system to deliver on what it promises is alarmingly   deficient. Currently it is estimated that between 70 and 90% of online advertising is transacted programmatically. There are also many hybrid versions of online buying which feature elements of both direct and programmatic buying. For the sake of keeping an impossibly complex system comprehensible, let's just agree that hybrid versions exist but let's not get into detailed descriptions of them.

The online advertising ecosystem is in reality impossibly complex. I am reproducing something here called a LUMAscape, named after LUMA Partners, the company that invented it.

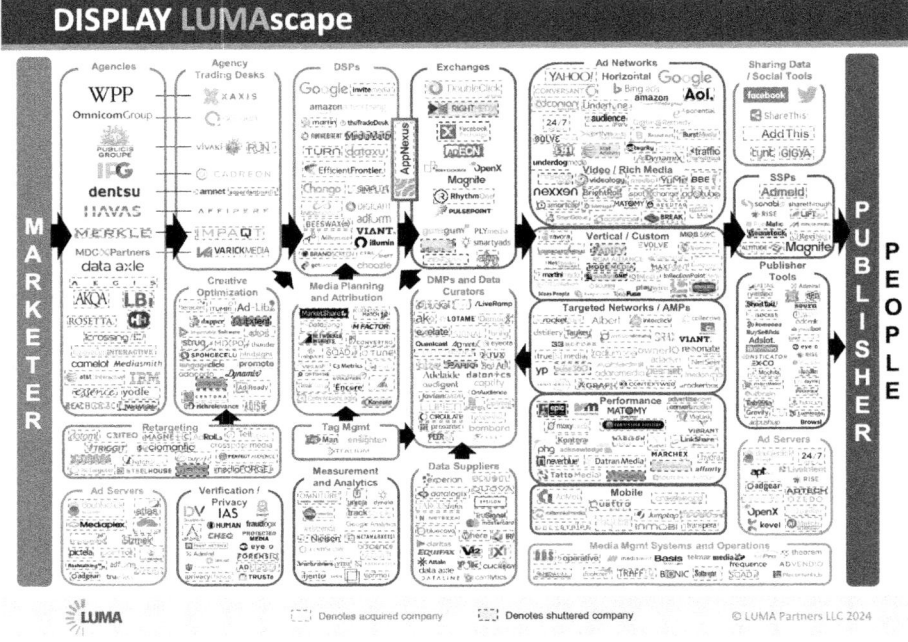

You don't have to fully comprehend it to get an idea of the insanely tortuous route a display ad may take from the time it leaves your desk to the time it appears on a website. As stated earlier, the system is so complex it is essentially incomprehensible.

I believe it was British media expert Irwin Gottlieb who said, *"In complexity there is margin."* When a system is complex, there is plenty of room for bad actors. Bad actors have more opportunity to insert themselves into the process, and therefore, more opportunity to act nefariously. There may be good actors who actually add value. And there is also room for unproductive actors to extract money while contributing little or nothing.

Complex systems also make it much more difficult for buyers to know where their money is going, who it is going to, what they are getting for it, or at what point it is disappearing.

Underlying the programmatic ad ecosystem is a process called real-time bidding (RTB.) RTB allows many advertisers to simultaneously bid on the same ad slot on a website as soon as a person arrives there. A computer driven online auction takes place in nanoseconds. The highest bid wins the auction, and the auction winner's ad is placed in the slot and, at least in theory, delivered to the person.

(As an aside, RTB is an unusually dangerous process which you will read about later in my chapter describing my talk to the European Parliament.)

Disneyland for Crooks

Just to get our blood pumping, let's look at a few key facts about online advertising. Then we'll come back in later chapters and get into some depth on these facts. I have gathered these facts from the most reliable sources available.

- According to a study by the Incorporated Society of British Advertisers (ISBA) and consultants PwC, while your ad is traveling from your desk to a website, half of what you paid for that ad is siphoned off by adtech middlemen.

- A report by the ANA (Association of National Advertisers) in 2023 claimed that 25% of programmatic ad dollars are wasted. Projecting this over the total spend on programmatic advertising would mean that over $130 billion is wasted. Let me emphasize that by 'wasted' the ANA doesn't mean that it is poorly conceived or executed. It means that the advertiser is being screwed out of 25% of what they think they have bought. As we progress, you will see why I believe this estimate is actually very low.

- According to Juniper Research, ad fraud alone cost advertisers $84 billion in 2023. They reported that 22% of all digital advertising spend was stolen by fraud. The ANA study mentioned above did not include ad fraud in its calculation. We will be discussing what ad fraud is and how it works in the next section.

- Juniper predicts that in 2024 ad fraud will reach $100 billion.

- The ANA says that about 15% of programmatic ad dollars are eaten up by MFAs (useless 'made for advertising' websites.) Again, I suspect the actual number is higher. Other reports have it at over 20%.

- Ads from an average programmatic campaign by a 'sophisticated' advertiser will appear on over 40,000 websites. This makes accurately monitoring an online campaign impossible. Nobody can do audits on 40,000 websites. And, as we'll see, it makes the programmatic ecosystem Disneyland for crooks.

- According to the ISBA report alluded to previously, 80% of the websites that programmatically purchased ads run on are 'non-premium' websites. Non-premium is a nice gentlemanly British way of saying 'crap.'

- Integral Ad Science (IAS) says that between 30 and 50% of display ads are non-viewable. Non-viewable means the ad loads outside the screen's viewable area; or the ad doesn't render in time for a viewer to see it; or multiple ads are stacked on one another; or one of several other factors that make the ad invisible to people looking at the page.

- According to the above-mentioned study by the ANA, only 36¢ out of every online ad dollar gets from an SSP (sell side platform) to a consumer.

- According to Lumen Research, only 9% of online ads get even one second of consumer attention.

Reports that agencies receive from suppliers, and reports marketers receive from agencies, and reports corporate management receives from their marketing departments about the reach, cost, and efficacy of their campaigns are highly unreliable. The Association of National Advertisers says that the programmatic media buying ecosystem is *"riddled with material issues including thin transparency, fractured accountability, and mind-numbing complexity."* According to the CEO of the ANA, *"We believe this lack of transparency is costing advertisers billions of dollars in waste."*

Two things are apparent from these facts. First, there are so many intertwined ways programmatic ad dollars are being siphoned off, stolen, and wasted, I am sure I must be double counting some of the bad stuff I've mentioned. Even programmatic advertising can't be more than 100% waste.

Second, whatever the true extent of waste is, it is staggering.

Let's sum up with a quote from the director-general of the ISBA, *"The market is damn near impenetrable."*

Your Disappearing Money

Now let's have a look at a specific example of how researchers found one type of waste in the programmatic ad ecosystem.

In 2021, the ISBA (the U.K. equivalent of the ANA) released a report on a study conducted over a two-year period by consultants PwC that laid out the absurd wastefulness of the adtech industry. The study was conducted to establish what component of an ad budget spent on programmatic online advertising actually results in *advertising.*

Fifteen major advertisers, including Disney, Unilever and Nestlé participated in the study as well as eight agencies, five DSPs, six SSPs, and twelve publishers. Also participating in the project were adtech companies Google DV360 and Ad Manager, Amazon Advertising, and the Rubicon Project. The PwC leader of the study said, *"It's important to realise that this study represents the most premium parts ... the highest profile advertisers, publishers, agencies and adtech."* Here are some highlights:

- Half of programmatic ad money was being siphoned off by the adtech industry before it reached publishers.

- According to the Financial Times, of the 50% of the budget that was siphoned off, about 1/3 of the dollars, *"were completely untraceable."* In some cases the untraceable costs were as high as 83%. This means the money just evaporated into the adtech black box without a trace.

- Only 12% of the ad dollars were completely transparent and traceable. An astounding 88% of dollars could not be traced from end to end.

Remember, this study only reported on the *highest quality tip of the iceberg* - the most premium end of the programmatic marketplace. Imagine what the numbers must be like in the rest of the adtech cesspool where most advertisers swim their laps.

In regard to this study, listen to this nonsense from an IAB (Interactive Advertising Bureau) spokesperson, *"...it is not a dark art and we shouldn't lose sight of the crucial role programmatic plays in supporting our ad-funded, open web."* As usual from these people, it is nonsense. The web is supported by advertising — not adtech, not programmatic horseshit, not dodgy middlemen.

And here's even worse news. Just because 50% of your ad budget is reaching publishers doesn't mean you're getting 50% of value from your ad investment. Let's not forget the fraud in the programmatic ecosystem. Once half your money escapes from the adtech jungle and gets to a publisher, it is still exposed to creepy publishers and fraudsters who hang around the programmatic playground.

As media fraud expert Dr. Augustine Fou says, " *... the 50% that makes it through to publishers could still be subject to fraud if that publisher is buying traffic and doing other shitty things like refreshing the page every 10 seconds, refreshing the ad slot every 2 seconds, stacking 10 ads on top of each other, loading 1,000 hidden ads in the background. The advertiser is still exposed to the potential of 100% fraud if that publisher is a fake site using fake traffic, and selling their inventory through the adtech plumbing.* "

In other words, the programmatic advertising ecosystem exposes advertisers to double jeopardy. First is the 50% of your investment you surrender to middlemen, then there are the other flavors of online jeopardy — fraud, MFAs, viewability issues, etc. Later on we'll see how much real advertising a programmatic ad dollar actually buys.

The adtech industry, and its supplicants in the agency business, will claim that adtech earns its money by adding value—by helping you find the most effective tactics for investing your advertising dollars. As we'll see this, too, is open to question. Adtech - as practiced in the programmatic ad ecosystem - not only does not necessarily add value, in many cases it degrades value.

What effect has the ISBA report had on the ad industry? Just like with ad fraud and privacy abuse, the ad industry is far too invested in the status quo, and too many people are making too much money, for the industry to do anything serious about the black hole of programmatic

Honey, Did You See My $140 Billion?

According to the ANA and PwC, 70% of advertising dollars spent in the U.S. on online programmatic advertising never reach a consumer.

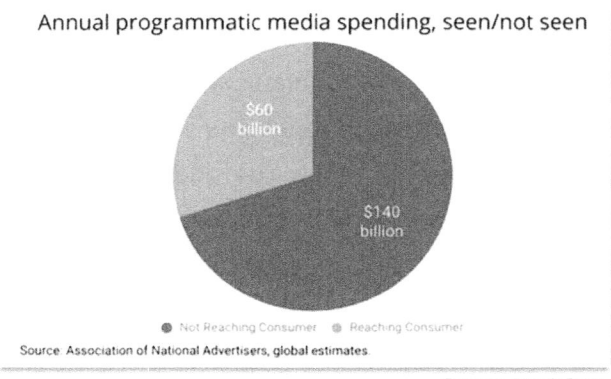

Annual programmatic media spending, seen/not seen

Source: Association of National Advertisers, global estimates

Source: MediaPost

Of $200 billion in annual programmatic ad spent in the US, $140 billion disappeared in "*ad fees, fraud, non-viewable impressions, non-brand-safe placements, and unknown allocations*" (by 'unknown allocations' you can substitute 'shit that no one can figure out.')

As a consequence, in 2021 the ANA announced they were commissioning an *"in-depth study of the programmatic media-buying ecosystem."*

For years the the ANA has been talking out of both sides of its mouth -- whining about the sleaze of the adtech industry but tripping in its underwear with cockamamie contradictory reports. We'll get to that later.

The implementation of the ANA's study was too little too late. By the time the ANA report was issued in 2023, the ISBA in the UK had already made headlines revealing the wasteful nature of the programmatic ad industry. The report, which took the ANA two years to release, was a non-event. All it did was verify what everyone with half a lobe already knew -- advertisers are being screwed.

One of the only interesting aspects of the ANA study was how the adtech industry stonewalled the ANA. According to Digiday, *"Vested interests from some of the industry's most powerful players have frustrated the project's earliest ambitions."*

Google, by far the largest player in online advertising, was particularly uncooperative. According to AdExchanger, there was *"a woeful gap in terms of vendor participants."* This is just a complicated way of saying that a whole lot of people in the programmatic supply chain are playing keep-away — working hard to keep the system as opaque as possible.

The ANA's EVP, Bill Duggan had this to say, *"We thought it would be to the benefit of all of the supply chain participants to be noted in the report....Everyone says they are supporters of transparency, until they're the ones asked to be transparent."*

What is Ad Fraud?

Ad fraud is a type of crime in which thieves use computer technology to steal money from businesses. The businesses think they are buying advertising, but they are actually buying nothing.

Ad fraud is found mainly in online advertising (display ads and online video ads) but in recent years has become a growing problem in web- delivered TV (also known as Connected TV or CTV) advertising. A study by DoubleVerify reported that in 2021, fraud schemes in CTV surged by 70%.

The reason ad fraud has become pervasive is twofold. First, to a large degree advertisers no longer buy advertising directly from the people who run the advertising. And second, the system by which they buy advertising is largely incomprehensible.

One of the key attributes of online advertising that makes it uniquely susceptible to fraud is, in the words of the CEO of the Association of National Advertisers, its "mind-numbing complexity." In fact, it is so complex it is indecipherable to almost everyone who participates in the system.

When we are talking about ad fraud we are not talking about fraud that is perpetrated on the public. We are talking about fraud that is going on within the advertising industry. In other words, an advertiser —let's say Coca-Cola—is paying $100 to buy advertising but is only getting $50 worth of advertising because $50 is being scraped by middlemen, fraudsters, and others as the ad moves through many hands on its way from Coke to a website.

I am not going to attempt to explain all the different types of fraud that exist because you have to be a computer scientist or software engineer to understand the terminology and activities that sit under the hood of online advertising to understand how some fraud types work. But here are brief descriptions of a few of the more understandable ones:

<u>Domain Spoofing</u>: Fraudsters attract ad dollars by creating websites that look identical to high-quality websites.

<u>Cookie Stuffing</u>: No, it's not the cream in an Oreo. Crooks drop cookies all over the place. When someone who's had a cookie dropped on them goes to an affiliate website, the cookie dropper gets paid for nothing.

<u>Click Injection</u>: Fraudsters trick you into installing malware on your computer. The malware goes all over the web clicking on things. Every time it clicks somewhere, someone gets paid.

Pixel Stuffing: It's not a tiny Thanksgiving side dish. A crook builds invisible one pixel 'ads', spreads hundreds of them (or more) on a web page. Each pixel is paid for by an advertiser as if it's a real ad.

Ad Stacking: Just like pixel stuffing, except the fraudster stacks ads one on top of another. They can't be seen, but the advertiser still pays.

Ad Injection: A fraudster substitutes his own ad for your ad but you pay anyway.

Click Farms: Criminals program hundreds or thousands of computers to do nothing but click on ads 24 hours a day for unscrupulous web publishers. Sometimes click farms use real people to sit and click all day, every day.

Click Hijacking: Fraudsters use malware to redirect clicks in an endless loop.

By the time this is published some of these frauds will be obsolete and new more potent fraud types will be invented.

The big picture looks like this: the way fraudsters take advantage of the vulnerability of the system is primarily by creating fake websites, fake audiences, and fake clicks. Crooks use software strings, called bots, to produce fake audiences and fake clicks. In 2020 web security company Barracuda Networks reported there was *more traffic on the web from malignant bots than there was from human beings.*

One important fact to understand is that bots can be created out of thin air. This means that fake audiences, and fake clicks can be created out of nothing by someone sitting at a keyboard.

Exploiting the programmatic advertising system is remarkably simple. You can become a successful ad fraudster with almost no technical know-how. And if you have technical know- how, the sky's the limit. According to Hewlett Packard Enterprises, ad fraud has both the highest potential for profitability and the lowest barrier to entry. This is a very bad combination.

In May of 2020 a reporter for CNBC set out to see how easy it is to become a card- carrying ad fraudster and attract paid advertising to a fully plagiarized website. With no particular tech skills she was able to scrape content from websites, plug the plagiarized content into an off-the-shelf website skeleton she found, get approved by ad networks, and attract legitimate advertisers like Kohl's, Wayfair, and Overstock. If someone with no technical training can become a functioning fraudster in a couple of days, imagine what the sophisticated tech monsters are doing.

Of course there are companies that sell security against ad fraud by claiming to be able to identify fraudulent activity. The problem is, these protections are marginally useful. The bad guys always seem to be three steps ahead of the good guys. One researcher who wanted to test the efficacy of fraud detection software directed 100% fake traffic that he had created to a website he also created. Then he hired one of the leading fraud detection companies to give him a report on his traffic. They reported that 83% of the traffic was legitimate.

Later on you will read how billions of ad bids went to the wrong places without fraud detection companies noticing a thing.

Bob Hoffman

How Large Is Ad Fraud?

Ad fraud is one of the largest frauds in history. Nobody knows the exact extent of ad fraud but several reputable studies peg it at over $80 to $100 billion annually. Here are some interesting stats on ad fraud.

According to Advertising Age magazine and Spider Labs, " *... an estimated 20% of (online) ad budgets globally (are) being snatched by fraudsters.* " If that number is right, in 2024 well over $100 billion will be lost to online ad fraud.

Juniper Research estimated 2023 ad fraud at $84 billion.

The Association of National Advertisers (ANA) in the U.S. has variously estimated 2022 ad fraud at $81 billion and $120 billion.

The World Federation of Advertisers reported that by 2025 advertising fraud may be the second largest source of criminal income on the planet, after drug trafficking.

Professor Roberto Cavazos, an economist who has studied business fraud for over 30 years says, *"the level of ad fraud is now staggering. The digital advertising sector has ... higher fraud rates than multi-trillion-dollar sectors."*

Cheq, a fraud detection company, says that online ad fraud has overtaken credit card fraud despite the fact that the credit card business is ten times the size of online advertising.

Kevin Frisch, the former head of performance marketing and consumer relations management at Uber says that one type of ad fraud called attribution fraud was headed toward eating $100 million of Uber's $150 million online ad budget: *"We turned off 2/3 of our spend ... and basically saw no change ... "*

Dr. Augustine Fou calculated that just one detected instance of fraud called "Fireball" could generate 30 billion fraudulent ad impressions a minute. He said, *"...fraud on such a massive scale is beyond belief."*

Why Is Ad Fraud Thriving?

By now you are probably asking yourself, "If we know ad fraud is massive, and we know how it's done, why is it thriving?" It's a damn good question. Let's have a look at some of the factors that keep it growing.

The Risk Factor

The first reason is probably the easiest to understand. With ad fraud, there is almost no risk. Prosecution for ad fraud is essentially non-existent. In fact, in many jurisdictions its status as a crime is not even clear.

A great deal of ad fraud, like so much web activity, is transnational. While the malefactors may be on one continent, the victims may be on another. The laws in one country may be quite different from another. The cultural concerns about fraud may be intense in one country and nowhere to be found in another. Does the government of Iran really worry about fraudsters in its jurisdiction who are extracting money from clueless American corporations? It is quite likely that hostile governments themselves are sponsoring some of the fraud.

Even within jurisdictions there is skepticism. Is it really a government's responsibility to babysit the foolish and irresponsible advertising investments of corporations? Some would say no. If corporations and trade organizations aren't even willing to acknowledge the seriousness of the problem and take vigorous action to protect and defend their own dollars, why should governments?

Perverse Incentives

All along the money chain, the incentives to acknowledge and attack ad fraud are missing. You would think that advertisers, who are the primary victims, would be heavily incentivized to do something about it. They are not.

The chief marketing officers of most corporations, who are responsible for marketing expenditures, have been promoting the benefits of online advertising to their stakeholders (CEO's, CFO's, boards) for years. It is not in their best interest to look like fools who have been taken to the cleaners and have wasted millions (in some cases tens and hundreds of millions) on fairy tales.

Here's a note I received from a very smart former ad agency executive I've known for years who went to work on the corporate marketing side:

"Now that I'm ... on the client side, I've noticed something: It's in nobody's interest for digital ad numbers to be true as long as they're

good. Whether that's 'reach', 'engagement' or whatever other idiotic measure they use.

"The client wants to see numbers go up every month, regardless of their value or truth. Same for the media planner and buyer. Ditto for the account team and the creative guys. No one will question the efficacy of the numbers because they love showing the CEO (who understands nothing about marketing) that we gained x number of followers, reached an additional y people, and z more people saw our 'content.'

Everybody is in on the con. None of the involved parties want anyone to examine the numbers as long as they're good. No one. It's pathetic."

Ad agency holding companies have invested heavily in adtech businesses. One would not be overly cynical to wonder if their enthusiasm for online advertising was driven in part by self-interest. According to Statista, on average over 64% of agency revenue comes from digital advertising.

There are also perverse incentives in ad agency and adtech compensation models. Most agencies are paid on volume, not quality. The more advertising they buy the more money they make. For the most part, they make the same commissions and fees whether they are buying fake audiences or real audiences, fake websites or real websites. For the most part, agencies receive the same compensation regardless of how much fraudulent advertising they are inadvertently buying. They make their commissions before the fraud.

It's not that the agencies are complicit with the fraudsters, it's just that they have no financial incentive to do very much to protect their clients' interests. Instead, they hire incompetent fraud detection companies to cover their asses.

Fraudsters have tremendous incentive to be aggressive. They can make large amounts of money. What incentives do agencies have to play defense? Are they going to make more money? No, it may even cost them money. A typical programmatic ad buy will include thousands of websites. It's much easier to employ fraud detection vendors who do perfunctory scans than to analyze the code behind ad activity on tens of thousands of websites.

Information Asymmetry

Throughout the programmatic money chain sellers have information that buyers don't have. What most advertisers don't understand is that the reports they get on traffic and clicks are often unreliable. These reports contend that visitors are real but they are not. As the World Federation of Advertisers says, *" ... reporting validates a visitor to be authentic, but it is actually fraudulent. "*

Advertisers have no choice but to rely on these questionable reports because the alternative is unworkable. Confirming the validity of a report on a programmatic media buy may entail doing forensic audits on tens of thousands of websites. No one can do this. And yet, believing one of the reports you get from a verification vendor is like believing your 16-year-old's explanation of how the car door got scratched.

Information asymmetry always leads to problems. People and organizations think they know things that they don't really know. Meanwhile people who have better information are in a position to take advantage of their information superiority.

Let's be blunt. Everything the adtech industry has ever told us about privacy and security has, in the fullness of time, been shown to be horseshit. They are largely incompetent, irresponsible, and dangerous.

On May 24, 2017, the Association of National Advertisers and its cyber-security consultants at White Ops announced that based on a study they had conducted, online ad fraud would drop 10% in 2017. The CEO of the ANA said, *"Marketers worldwide are successfully adopting strategies and tactics to fight digital ad fraud ... "* Just one week later, Check Point, a software technology company, announced a previously undetected fraud operation called "Fireball". Check Point reported that Fireball had infected 250 million computers and 20% of corporate networks worldwide. Forbes said, *" ... [it] might be the biggest Android ad fraud ever."*

There are very few in the marketing and advertising world who understand the intricacies of programmatic systems. There are even fewer who can go under the hood of a programmatic media buy and analyze activities to understand what is real and what is not. There are even fewer who have the time, energy, or inclination to analyze the code on the tens of thousands of websites. In fact, there are none.

A famous case involves Chase bank. They were advertising on 400,000 sites every month. Imagine having to analyze the audience and click activities on 400,000 sites to understand what is really going on. On a hunch, they reduced the number of monthly sites to 5,000 (a reduction of almost 99%) and saw no difference in performance. An astounding number of the sites they were buying programmatically were worthless.

The bad guys are constantly looking for ways to attack whatever defenses the good guys can put up. The good guys are always playing defense. To understand this better, let's take a brief detour and talk about basketball and hockey. Basketball is a game with rules that greatly favor offense. If you're playing defense and you breathe too hard on your opponent you're called for a foul. Consequently, basketball is a game with a lot of offense. You usually have to score 100 points to win.

Hockey is the opposite. In hockey, the defensive player has some very substantial advantages. You can pretty much maim or kill your opponent and not be penalized, as long as you don't do it with a machete. The result is that four goals are often enough to win a game. Ad fraud is like basketball. All the advantage is to the offense—that is, the fraudsters. The criminals have the information, the good guys are searching for it.

The gullibility of advertisers is beyond explanation. I guess they must think there is someone somewhere who's looking after their interests. There isn't. Their agencies aren't protecting them. As long as clients keep pressing agencies for lower media costs they'll continue to use programmatic methods for buying cheaper and crappier media. Unlike traditional media where lower costs-per-thousand (CPMs) usually indicate efficient buying, in digital media lower CPMs often indicate you are wasting money buying bots and MFA websites.

Their CMO's aren't protecting them. As we'll see in the next chapter, it's often not in their best interest.

The 4A's (American Association of Advertising Agencies) isn't protecting them. The 4A's has become a lapdog for the big six advertising holding companies, and the big six are feasting at the online ad buffet.

The IAB (Interactive Advertising Bureau) is a cruel joke.

The ANA (Association of National Advertisers) has been covering-up fraud for years. We'll get to that soon.

So who's going to protect dazed and confused brands from themselves? Ad agencies have been particularly negligent in educating their clients about how much they may be losing to ad fraud. Online advertising spending constitutes about 2/3 of all ad spending. No one wants to disturb that golden goose. Meanwhile advertisers, seduced by the unrelenting hype about the miracle of online advertising, can't get enough of the stuff. One can only wonder how strongly ad fraud remediation would be pursued if the beneficiaries were being punished instead of rewarded.

Finally, everyone thinks it's the other guy that's getting screwed. You see, 'we have systems in place that protect us... blah blah blah...it's the other guys that are getting the shaft.' Everyone thinks it's the other guy.

Programmatic Poop Funnel

In 2022 I created something I called the Programmatic Poop Funnel. Using the ad industry's most reliable sources, I attempted to demonstrate the value of what $1 spent on programmatic advertising actually bought in terms of actual ads viewed by actual people. The answer was 3¢. I traced a dollar spent for programmatically-bought display advertising on its exciting journey from your pocket to the bank accounts of middlemen, con men, crooks, and the Bermuda Triangle.

In the two years since I created the funnel, I'm sure some of the numbers have changed. But I'm equally sure that those that changed for the better are at least offset by those that have changed for the worse. I'm pretty sure the total effect is pretty much the same and you're probably getting equal 'value' for your ad buck.

It turns out that the programmatic apparatus has been wonderfully efficient for the lads and lassies in the adtech industry. Not so efficient for losers like you and me. Let's see how it's working..

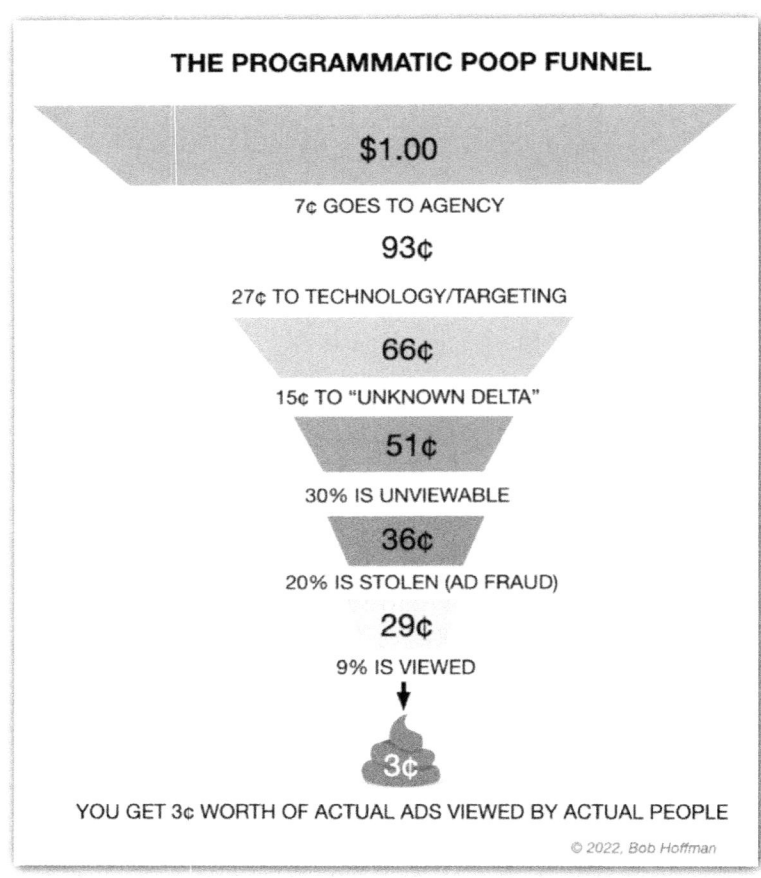

In 2022 I estimated that $1 spent on programmatic advertising bought 3¢ worth of real ads seen by real humans

1. You start with a dollar to spend

2. On average, your agency gets a 7¢ fee

3. Technology and targeting fees take another 27¢ (DSPs, SSPs, and WTFs)

4. 15¢ mysteriously disappears into the "unknown delta." No one knows where the "unknown delta" is. My guess? North Korea, Atlantis, or Boca Raton.

5. 30% of the ads you buy won't be viewable

6. About 20% of the stuff you buy will be fraudulent

7. Only 9% of the display ads that actually run will be viewed by a real person for even a second.

8. Copywriter math notwithstanding, it looks like your dollar bought you 3¢ of real display ads viewed by real human people.

As I'm sure you know, no one in the comical online metrics business can agree on anything. I have taken the numbers in the above illustration from the most reliable sources I could find:

- The first four items come from the ISBA (Incorporated Society of British Advertisers) and PwC's, Programmatic Supply Chain Transparency Study

- Item 5 comes from Integral Ad Science

- Item 6 comes from AdAge and Spider Lab's report, *"Combating Ad Fraud in the Age of COVID-19"*

- Item 7 comes from Lumen Research.

It's important to note that the ISBA study alluded to above only reported on the *highest quality* tip of the iceberg -- the most premium end of the programmatic marketplace. These are the 20% of buyers that are presumed to be the most skillful. Even at that premium end, only 12% of the ad dollars were completely transparent and traceable.

How many people actually view a display ad? The IAB defines a view as 50% of an ad's pixels seen for one second. Huh? Even by this absurd standard only 9% of online ads are 'viewed.'

Enormous Demand for Garbage

It's very hard to understand why no one in marketingland seems terribly concerned about the billions of dollars that are being stolen annually by fraudsters. You would think that with reputable organizations and researchers reporting somewhere in the neighborhood of $100 billion being stolen annually there would be howling and screaming coming out of marketing organizations. And yet... crickets. How can this be?

One important factor in the continuing growth of a wasteful, corrupt system is that it is beneficial to a great many of the very people who should be policing it. It turns out there is an enormous demand for garbage. Garbage makes marketers look good. Lemme explain.

The personal interest of a marketer is not necessarily in alignment with the interests of the brand he or she is employed by. Within the marketing industry, and within corporations, there are perverse incentives at work.

As we know, CMO is a very insecure job. Reports claim that the average life of a CMO is somewhere in the neighborhood of 24 months. According to Harvard Business Review *"Eighty percent of CEOs say they don't trust or are unimpressed by their CMOs."* This is not good.

I am fond of ridiculing CMOs. So many of them seem to be flat tires who have memorized a lexicon of marketing clichés and just repeat them endlessly. My taunting of CMO's aside, I have to admit that it's a near impossible job, and I wouldn't do it for all the empty real estate in the metaverse.

One of a CMO's most difficult jobs is managing an advertising budget. If you are a big brand marketing honcho there are innumerable ways to piss away millions of ad dollars. Obviously, wasting millions of ad dollars by buying fake advertising is a terrible thing for a brand or a business. But it's not so terrible for the personal interest of an individual. To understand why, let's first agree on a couple of unpleasant realities:

1. A marketer's first priority is to keep his/her job.

2. Trying to tease out the effect of advertising on brand health from all the other business variables (product quality, sales force competence, operations, design, distribution, pricing, competitor activity, economic conditions, etc.) is a never-ending brain destroyer.

This is where ad fraud and perverse incentives come in. Numbers are the best friend of a CMO or anyone else who has to justify advertising expenditures. With numbers, you can demonstrate to the other C-Something-Os in your organization and to your board that you are using the money wisely and effectively.

Ad fraud provides marketers with fabulous numbers. Buying bots and other crappy ad inventory is wonderfully cheap. It makes reach look enviable and CPMs look wonderful. And to top it off, bots click relentlessly on ads creating the illusion of 'performance.'

In a rational world, fraud detection software would not allow marketers to accept bogus metrics as real. But let's not kid ourselves. As we'll see in the upcoming chapter entitled "Worldwide Hackathon" in 2021 it was found that Russian hackers had been outfoxing the US's most secure cybersecurity defenses including the military's Cyber Command, the National Security Agency (NSA), and the Department of Homeland Security. Do you really think the fraud dudes aren't giggling at the defenses thrown up by ad fraud venders? So here's the conflict. Ad fraud makes marketers look good and balance sheets look bad.

Remember garbage may stink, but it's very cheap. The metrics generated by garbage sites, garbage buys, and garbage reports provide marketers with fabulous nonsense that they can wave in front of their overlords. When you've been promoting the success of your marketing strategy for years, it becomes very uncomfortable to suddenly say, "Oh, by the way, we've been getting screwed." It's much pleasanter to say…

"Look how many people we reached!"

"Look how many clicks we got!"

"Look how low our CPMs are!"

But don't look too close, because it's all bullshit.

Am I saying that marketing people are irresponsible and too selfishly motivated to be trusted? Not exactly. What I'm saying is that to many marketers the personal incentive for unmasking the extent of fraud in the online ad ecosystem is very small, but the incentive for turning a blind eye is very high.

Billions of Mistakes. No One Noticed

Among the frustrations of digital advertising, I think it's fair to say that near the top is not knowing who and what to believe. While online advertising technology was supposed to provide us with near perfect data on who we were reaching, where we were reaching them, and what it was costing, twenty years later we find that the extent of uncertainty about what is happening with our advertising money online is staggering.

Ironically, non-digital (or, if you prefer, off-line) advertising is often able to provide more certainty about what we are paying, who we are paying it to, and what we are buying. If you buy an ad in The New York Times you can open a copy of The Times and see your ad there. If you buy a spot on Monday Night Football, you can watch the game and see your ad. But if you do a programmatic ad campaign online it is virtually impossible to ascertain what you have bought or where it has run. Every time the the ad appears it appears as a result of a real-time auction. You have no idea where your ad is going to run. Even if you want to monitor 40,000 websites you can't.

Consequently there is no way for any company's management - no matter how sophisticated they think they are - to have first-hand knowledge of what is actually going on with all their digital ad spending. Instead, they must rely on reports they get from the systems used to sell the ads (often SSPs), the systems used to buy the ads (often DSPs), the people at agencies who gather the information and consolidate it, fraud and security detection vendors, and the people in the marketing departments who evaluate and vet the reporting.

In other words, because of the arcane nature of the online advertising ecosystem, there is a chain of reporting that is the only way for businesses to get information on how their online advertising budgets are actually being spent.

The exasperating part of this is that there is also no way for the recipients of the reports to verify the accuracy of the reports themselves. So not only are the actions of the programmatic advertising system opaque, the reports that presumably validate the actions are also opaque.

But sometimes, just by chance, lightening strikes and it becomes clear to everyone what is actually going on. Such a thing happened a while back. An accidental research project occurred which unambiguously demonstrated how little we can trust the competence of the experts who report to us and are charged with informing and protecting us from the opaque activities of the programmatic ad system.

In the clearest possible terms, we non-computer scientists, non-software engineers, and non-adtech experts got an explicit look at the inner workings of the people we rely on to inform us and protect us in this mysterious world. And it was alarming.

Two researchers named Krzysztof Franaszek and Braedon Vickers, working at a company called Adalytics, stumbled upon an error. They discovered that Gannett Publishing had unintentionally been publishing online ads in the wrong places. This chance discovery has led to a uniquely disturbing set of revelations.

Gannett owns the USA Today website. It also owns hundreds of small community news sites. For nine months Gannett had been conducting billions of ad auctions for space on the USA Today site, but had accidentally been sending bid-winning ads to the other websites it owns. In other words, for nine months advertisers like Sears, Nike, Adidas, Ford, State Farm, Starbucks, Kia and Marriott had been paying for and thinking their ads ran on the USA Today site, but actually they may have run on the websites of the Ruidoso News, a biweekly news outlet in New Mexico, or the Lebanon Daily News in Lebanon, PA.

The question is this: How can the ads of winning bids from billions of ad auctions wind up in the wrong places without...

...a single brand noticing that their ads weren't where they were supposed to be?

...a single agency knowing what they were buying?

...a single fraud detection company, or media verification firm unearthing the fact that all these ads went to the wrong places?

According to The Wall Street Journal, at least fifteen different adtech companies that were part of the chain of buying, selling, and verification for Gannett had enough information to see what was going on. Not a single one of these companies discovered or reported it. As far as can be told, not a single company even understood what they were looking at.

Companies who had the information at hand were some of the biggest in the adtech field: Integral Ad Science, Double Verify, and Oracle's MOAT. Of particular interest is Integral Ad Science. Not only do these 'scientists' specialize in reporting fraud, according to the Journal...*"Gannett pays Integral Ad Science for insights on its traffic and metrics related to its advertising... Data gathered by the researchers and reviewed by the Journal showed that Integral Ad Science received information revealing the Gannett discrepancy thousands of times. Integral Ad Science didn't inform Gannett of the phenomenon... and didn't inform its advertiser clients, according to media buyers."*

Several adtech companies that represent sellers on Gannett's websites including Pubmatic, TripleLift, and Criteo had enough information to know what was going on. Several companies that represent buyers on Gannett's sites, including Google's Display & Video 360, Publicis' Conversant, The Trade Desk, and Media Math also should have known. According to the Journal, *"Each of them had enough information to raise concerns about the publisher's auctions..."*

Ads from winning companies of billions of ad auctions went awry and all along the adtech chain of responsibility companies that had the information necessary to see what was going on didn't know what was going on. Not a single brand noticed that their ads were not where they were supposed to be. Not a single media buyer noticed that their ads were misplaced. And for nine months we can only assume that these 'sophisticated' advertisers were receiving fictitious reports about the nature of their programmatic buy.

If these leading adtech companies don't have the competence to discover enormous numbers of honest mistakes from a company who is *not* trying to deceive them, what level of confidence can we have in their ability to identify the work of fraudsters who *are* trying to deceive them? I think we know the answer.

Every once in a while serendipity strikes and shows us in unambiguous terms exactly what is going on. You could not design a clearer, more honest test of the competence and credibility of the programmatic advertising apparatus.

We now have alarming and incontrovertible evidence - due to an accident - that we cannot trust the adtech ecosystem, and most vividly, we cannot trust the information we get from the people we pay to protect us from the uncertainties of the programmatic ad system.

In graphic terms, online advertisers just take wads of money, throw it up in the air, and believe any horseshit they are fed about where it lands. As Dr. Augustine Fou said, *"..it appears that no one ...in the entire programmatic supply chain detected the 'error...'*

None of the ad exchanges and DSPs caught this. None of the fraud detection tech companies caught this. None of the TAG "certified against fraud" companies caught this. None of the ad tech companies with MRC accreditation caught this. *"If Gannett didn't correct this 'error,' and the researchers didn't document...the issue, how long would this have continued?"*

Bad guys do this all the time with the intent of fooling the system. If good guys do it accidentally with no intent to fool, but still can't be detected by the people who are supposed to be guarding the jewels, what chance do they have against the bad guys?

Fou adds...*"Gannett's mess-up exposes the elephant in the room...but the question is WHICH elephant was it? That no one is looking? That fraud detection tech doesn't work? That fraud detection worked but everyone ignored it anyway? This went on for 9 months and across billions of bid requests. Which fu*king elephant was it?"*

You truly cannot make this up.

The Google/YouTube Scandal

Google has a product called Google Video Partners. It extends Google's reach and its ability to sell advertising placements to marketers. Google owns YouTube. Google Video Partners places a marketer's advertising on videos running on third party sites (in other words, not on YouTube's primary site) and guarantees quality placements on quality sites.

Google charges advertisers a premium price for advertising through its Google Video Partners network. While an advertiser might pay $5 per 1,000 completed views on a low quality video network, advertisers can pay up to twenty times that - $100 per 1,000 completed views - on the Google Video Partners network. This is because of the supposedly higher quality of the media.

There's just one problem. Google Video Partners ain't what it says it is. According to a report in The Wall Street Journal, research conducted by Adalytics covering billions of ad placements by over 1,000 brands between 2020 and 2023, showed that 80% of the time Google violated its own standards for Google Video Partners in placing ads on the network.

The 100+ page report on the scandal, written by Adalytics head Dr. Krzysztof Franaszek, was first reported in the Wall Street Journal in the US, and the Financial Times in the UK. Dr. Franaszek has written several brilliant reports exposing the corruption and incompetence in the adtech industry.

He was the researcher who discovered the Gannett/USA Today screw-up. In 2021 he reported on Google serving ads on Russia-linked websites after the sites were placed on the US sanctions list. The startling thing about Franaszek's work is that it is being done by an advertising outsider. He is by training a bio-medical researcher with a PhD in computational biology from Cambridge.

The question his findings raise is why it takes one person, like Franaszek or like the reporters who cover the ad industry, to uncover the corruption, fraud, and incompetence in our industry while our 'leaders' who are supposed to protect advertisers from corruption, and our holding company heads who have thousands of employees and billions in resources seem to know nothing.

I think the answer is clear. The advertising industry has become a wholly owned subsidiary of Adtech International. The adtech industry has subverted the integrity of the ad industry with years of fraud, corruption and incompetence. But no one dares challenge them.

The advertising industry is responsible for stewarding hundreds of billions of our clients' dollars on digital advertising. The Google/ YouTube scandal has once again demonstrated that we are not fit for purpose.

Media directors and media buyers who are supposed to be experts in analyzing the quality of media opportunities are apparently just animatrons who don't know what they are buying, who they are buying it from, where it is running, or what value it has. They take it on trust that the goods that are being sold to them by the adtech people are real. The Google Video Partners scandal is compelling evidence that some of the largest media buyers in the world have no idea what they're actually buying. They feed cash into the programmatic slot machine and cross their fingers..

As in all cases where adtech shenanigans have been uncovered, the uproar over the Google Video Partners racket soon died down. The agencies issued their lame excuses about how "we have systems in place..." marketing officers issued pathetic demands for their money back. The people who were supposed to represent and protect advertisers - the ANA, the 4As - continued to hide under their desks.

As always, in a few weeks the whole performance art of outrage evaporated. All the feckless experts who were demanding to see the manager will be found at Cannes sipping rosé on the Google yacht.

Forbes' Con Job

In online advertising nothing is what it appears to be. Adalytics made headlines once again with a report showing how Forbes online magazine had been screwing advertisers for years. Advertisers thought that ad campaigns they were buying from Forbes were running on Forbes website. Silly them.

Instead many ad campaigns were running on a bullshit look-alike MFA (made for advertising) website Forbes had created. The url of Forbes real website is https://www.forbes.com. Forbes created another website with url www3.forbes.com which was an MFA site. Unbeknownst to many advertisers, their ads were running on the bogus website where almost no one went, but they were paying Forbes regular ad prices.

Why would Forbes do this? According to The Drum, *"While a reader on Forbes's primary domain usually encounters between 3 to 10 ads throughout an article, viewers of www3.forbes.com might see over 200 ads during a single page view."*

You don't have to be an MBA to figure out that putting 200 ads on a page yields a lot more cash than 3. And you don't have to be a CMO to figure out that a page with 200 ads and no audience is a world class waste of money.

The advertisers conned by Forbes were not clueless idiots from Cheap Charlie's Discount Plumbing Supplies, these were clueless idiots from Microsoft, Disney, Ford, Johnson & Johnson, Mercedes Benz, Oracle, Fidelity, Marriott, Ford, United Airlines, Omnicom, Publicis, Havas, IPG, Dentsu, and GroupM. Along with hundreds of other, ya know, 'sophisticated' marketers.

According to the Wall Street Journal, *"The finding shines a light on the opacity of the digital-ad market, where brands frequently have to play whack-a-mole to keep their ad budgets from being wasted."* The Journal also reported that, *"All six major ad-agency holding companies —WPP, Omnicom, Publicis, Interpublic Havas and Dentsu -- bought ads that ran on that site. Those brands and ad-holding companies either declined to comment or didn't respond to requests for comment."* Lots of integrity there.

World's Clumsiest Cover-Up

In one of the most ludicrous, incompetent cover-up capers in advertising history, the Association of National Advertisers (ANA) has been guilty of giving their constituents false information about ad fraud for years. Let's have a look at what they've been up to.

In May of 2022, the ANA sent out a newsletter written by their Director of Research and Innovation which reported that in 2022 ad fraud was going to rise to cost advertisers between $81 and $120 billion.

The following ANA table shows that in 2022 fraud would cost advertisers $120 billion. It shows that it would cost advertisers $20 billion from app install farms and SDK spoofing, $35 billion from click spam and ad stacking, and $65 billion from click injection. For a total of $120 billion.

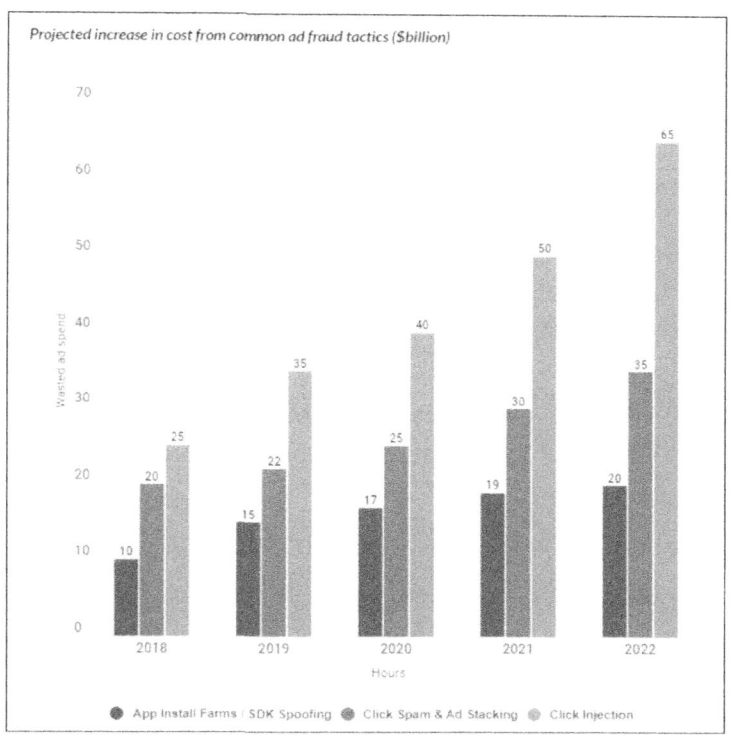

Projected increase in cost from common ad fraud tactics ($billion)

App Install Farms / SDK Spoofing   Click Spam & Ad Stacking   Click Injection

All of those estimates were exquisitely out of line with previous statements the ANA had made about ad fraud. Their history on this subject is ludicrous. In 2019 they said that the, *" ... war on ad fraud is succeeding"* and that ad fraud would amount to $5.8 billion in 2019. Here's part of a press release in which this claim was featured...

Report From ANA And White Ops Shows War On Ad Fraud Is Succeeding

Measures Designed to Block Fraudulent Impressions Are Working

PHOENIX (May 1, 2019) — Economic losses due to bot fraud are expected to total $5.8 billion globally this year, but for the first time ever more fraud will be stopped in 2019 than will succeed, according to the fourth Bot Baseline report from White Ops and the ANA (Association of National Advertisers).

The monetary losses, while significant, are an improvement over the $6.5 billion reported in the previous study released in 2017. The 11 percent decline in two years is particularly noteworthy considering that digital ad spending increased by 25.4 percent between 2017 and 2019.

Astoundingly, the 2022 newsletter estimated that fraud in 2019 had actually amounted to $72 billion, not the $5.8 billion reported in the press release above.

Put yourself in the shoes of the ANA. Your 'Director of Research and Innovation' has just posted a newsletter that contradicted everything you've told your constituents about ad fraud. What do you do?

Right! You disappear the newsletter. The next day the newsletter evaporated from the web. When you tried to access it, you got this message:

Membership   Events   Resources   Committees

Oops...

We're sorry, but the page you requested could not be found. Our technical support staff has been notified.

Try our site search to locate specific information or resources.

In the interim, please feel free to use our site search to help find what you are looking for. Or, if you want to search for a specific resource, video, or industry insight, search our Insights Library.

If you have any additional questions, you can also contact us.

This notification claimed that the page "could not be found" and that the ANA's technical staff "had been notified." It was a lie. The truth is they took down the newsletter because it was an embarrassment and emblematic of the incompetence and duplicity that have characterized the ANA's cover- up of ad fraud. The report was buried and disappeared from the web.

It's amazing how this document "could not be found" by the people who published it, but could be found by a dumbass copywriter. I have reproduced it on the next page.

The ANA is the primary trade group responsible for looking after the interests of the country's largest advertisers—Coke, Nike, GM, Budweiser, P&G, McDonald's, and just about every other substantial brand you can think of. But instead of doing their job, they have spent years tap-dancing and double-talking their way around what is costing companies billions of dollars every year. Instead of being honest with their constituents, the ANA is tripping in its underwear pretending ad fraud is under control.

No one knows the exact extent of ad fraud. Sadly, there is no International Registry of Fraud where criminals report their stolen gains. But as the representative association of most of the world's largest advertisers, the ANA needs to get its story straight. They have a responsibility to be honest with their constituents, with the business community, and with the public. On the next page you will find the document that "could not be found" by the ANA.

Sometimes it's hard to comprehend the meaning of large numbers. Here's some context. If the ANA's Director of Research and Innovation was correct, and ad fraud is stealing $120 billion a year from advertisers, ad fraud is as big a business as Coca-Cola, Nike, and McDonald's combined.

ANA's 'Lost' Report

This is the fraud report the ANA issued and then claimed "could not be found."

Worldwide Hackathon

In 2020, it was revealed that Russia had hacked 250 U.S. Government agencies. These hacks went undetected by our most sophisticated cybersecurity defenses including the military's Cyber Command, the National Security Agency, and the Department of Homeland Security. This alarming development must lead us to reevaluate everything we think we know about ad fraud.

It is folly to believe that hackers who can penetrate systems protected by the U.S. military's Cyber Command, the National Security Agency, and the Department of Homeland Security without detection cannot penetrate adtech systems.

There are governments in the world with both very sophisticated technology operations, and economies that would massively benefit from the addition of billions of dollars. If the Cyber Command, the NSA, and the Department of Homeland Security can be fooled, I don't think it's a stretch to assume that fraud detection software can also be fooled. Consequently, if state-sponsored hackers are fiddling the adtech ecosystem, it's likely that no one is detecting it.

It would be amazing if state-sponsored cyber criminals didn't view the adtech marketplace as ridiculously easy pickings and even more delicious since there are no consequences for being caught.

If state-sponsored penetration of adtech systems exists, the fraud detection companies should be considered seriously overmatched. And, of course, the bold assertions of trade organizations, agencies or marketers are no more reliable than those of the fraud detection companies they get their intelligence from.

While we know that criminals and criminal organizations are active in stealing money from the adtech systems, we don't know if governments are. In light of recent revelations, however, it seems highly likely that state-sponsored cyber operations would be powerfully attracted to the hundreds of billions of dollars the adtech ecosystem is unwittingly dangling in front of them. If so, ad fraud is probably a lot harder to detect and a lot larger than anyone thinks it is

Perfecting Incompetence

There are several different frightening stories to be told about programmatic advertising. The first story is about lying, cheating, and fraud. The second story is equally compelling. It is about the astounding incompetence that is everywhere to be found in the digital advertising ecosystem.

Let's take a minute here to recap some of what the research has shown us:

We'll start with the transparency reports from the ISBA in the UK, and the ANA in the U.S. In both cases it was shown that about 50¢ of every programmatic ad dollar was evaporating into the black box of fees, commissions, 'unknown deltas' and who knows where. And the shocking thing was that agencies and marketing leaders didn't know this. It's not like they weren't warned by researchers and adweasels. They just simply refused to exercise due diligence.

Additionally, there is fraud. For years holding companies, trade groups, and brand marketing executives have been obfuscating about the true size and nature of the beast.

Next we have just plain incompetence. The scandal involving Gannett Publishing showed that for nine months enormous numbers of ads for some of the world's largest brands including Sears, Nike, Adidas, Ford, State Farm, Starbucks, Kia and Marriott ran in the wrong places and no one knew.

The media buyers for the agencies didn't know.

The marketing people at the brand didn't know.

Not a single fraud detection company or media auditing firm indicated that they knew.

Presumably, each of these brands were getting reports during the nine month period telling them how beautifully their media buy was performing.

Then we have Google Video Partners scandal. For years Google was cheating hundreds of organizations including: The United States government; the European Parliament; JPMorgan Chase; American Express; Macy's; Disney; Best Buy; Mercedes-Benz; General Motors; McDonald's; IBM and Ford. Agencies that transacted business with Google Video Partners apparently had no idea what was going on included Interpublic; Dentsu; Publicis; Omnicom; WPP; Havas and Horizon. Once again, not a single agency, media buyer, CMO, fraud detection or media auditing company knew. Not one took the time or effort to find out where their money was going. One can only wonder what these people think their jobs are?

Let's end this with the MFA (made for advertising) scam site generated by Forbes that has been around since 2017. Agency networks that gladly put their clients money into this sewer - without having the slightest idea it was a scam - included Omnicom, Publicis, Havas, IPG, Dentsu, and GroupM. There are undoubtedly thousands of other MFA sites that these agencies know nothing about.

Sadly, we have no idea how many scam artists are stealing from advertisers every day of the year by way of the programmatic advertising system. All we know is that every time a conscientious researcher does a deep dive, they come up covered in sleaze.

There's one thing we know for sure. The people who are supposed to know what's going on don't. If we had set out to create a system that would guarantee marketers would be cheated relentlessly, we could not have done a better job.

Conspiracy of Silence

For several years, the advertising industry has been engaged in a conspiracy to deceive its clients and the public about online advertising.

It is not the kind of conspiracy you get when bad people get together to plot a crime. It is the kind of conspiracy you get when frightened people individually decide it is safer to keep their mouths and minds shut and keep on keepin' on.

For the last few years we have been flooded with scandals and revelations about corruption, fraud, and lies in the online advertising ecosystem. The terribly damning part is that there are only two possibilities: Either agencies are remarkably stupid and don't know what is going on, or they know and are keeping quiet. It's hard to decide which is worse.

Not a single one of the scandals involving online media has been brought to light by a media agency. Not one. Let's put this another way — not one of the scandals about online media were exposed by the people whose *job it is* to scrutinize online media.

Agencies, particularly media agencies, are as close to the online media industry as you can get. They are supposedly analyzing online media twenty-four hours a day. They are responsible for seeing to it that hundreds of billions of online advertising dollars are spent properly every year. They work very closely with media. They have the facts at their fingertips. They are assessing online media opportunities on behalf of their clients every day. How can it be that reporters and researchers, who are not trained in media, have not nearly the resources or access, and have no expertise in analyzing media, are able to sniff out scandal after scandal while the 'experts' are not able to do so? It is not possible. It doesn't even pass the giggle test.

As one very highly regarded media analyst commented to me, *"Agency bigwigs are notoriously paranoid and fearful. There's a strong code of silence."*

If it were left to the leaders of the ad industry, we would know nothing about any of the appalling stories documented in this book. By being ignorant of, or concealing, knowledge of deceit and dishonesty in online media, the ad industry has failed at one of its most consequential responsibilities – being trustworthy stewards of their clients' money.

But let's not be coy. Ad agencies are in bed with the adtech industry. Two thirds of their income is reported to be coming from online media. One can only wonder what additional sleaze the media 'experts' might know of and are keeping quiet about.

Every week there are alarming reports of fraud, corruption, privacy abuse, and security failures and we just shrug our shoulders and duck for cover. By being lapdogs to the corrupt and dangerous online media we are quickly squandering what's left of our credibility. We are on the wrong side of history and will continue to stay there until the silent conspiracy to protect the adtech industry ends.

How to Protect Yourself

Here are a few very simple things to do if you are determined to buy online advertising.

- Buy directly from quality publishers or quality publisher networks. Stay away from open ad networks and programmatic buying.

- Do not trust any reports you get from your agency. It's not that the agencies are corrupt, it's just that they get their data mostly from their suppliers, who are unreliable.

- Do not rely on reports from the major legacy fraud detection or ad verification suppliers. They have been shown to be unreliable.

- Do not rely on seals of approval or badges from organizations that supposedly vet websites for legitimacy.

- Question everything about a proposed media buy. The most important question to ask is: "How do you know this?"

- If you spend substantially on online advertising, work with a trusted consultant. I am not in the habit of making recommendations on suppliers, but if you've read this book you know who I trust and who I don't.

My Talk at the EU Parliament

In 2023 I was honored to be invited to Brussels to give a talk to members of the European Parliament on the dangers of ad fraud and online tracking. Here's what I had to say.

Good afternoon.

In my brief time today I would like to describe to you why I believe the adtech industry and the online advertising industry as they are currently configured are a danger to individuals and a danger to democratic societies. And why I believe it is important for legislative and regulatory bodies to take further action to curtail some of the practices that are harming both individuals and society.

First we need to acknowledge that advertising is essential to the free internet as we currently know it. People love the web. On average each if us spends about six hours a day online. The web gives us free entertainment, free information, and free communication. None of this would be possible without advertising. Advertising provides the financing for most of the web resources that we utilize every day.

But online advertising has an unnecessary and dangerous dark side. It is called tracking. Tracking is the process by which advertisers, online website publishers, and online media have the ability to know everywhere we go and everything we do on the web. Some call it tracking. Some call it surveillance. Some call it spying. It doesn't matter what you call it — it is a menace.

The adtech industry is capable of knowing every click we make, every site we visit, and where we are located at any time. In its worst moments, adtech knows who we are talking to and what we are saying. They can infer who our friends are, what our interests are, what our sexual preferences are, what our political leanings are, and where we are at any moment. They use this information in two ways: to sell us things, and to re-sell this information to other marketers.

Today I will talk about two of the most serious problems that this creates. First is the peril to individuals and society. Second is ad fraud. While on the surface, these may appear to be very different problems, beneath the surface they are both to a substantial degree manifestations of the online ad industry's original sin - tracking.

Here are some of the problems that the current version of adtech have created...

- Tracking, and the unrelenting collection, sharing, and selling of personal information about us is a danger to individuals. The worst governments in history have been the ones that abused the privacy of its citizens by following them everywhere, listening to their private conversations, and compiling secret files on them.

Today it is the marketing industry that is engaged in these practices. The KGB, the Gestapo, and the Stasi could only dream of having the depth of information about citizens that Google, Facebook, and other adtech companies have. According to a report by the Irish Council for Civil Liberties, people in Europe have their online behavior and location broadcast to thousands of companies and organizations around the world 197 billion times a day. Google alone sends this data to 4,698 organizations around the world, including Russia and China. There is no control over this data once it is sent.

A report to the British Parliament asserted that by the time an average child in Europe is 13-years-old, the adtech industry has 72 million data points on that child. We would never accept this level of spying on us by governments, but for some reason we have learned to accept it by marketers.

- Next, tracking is a danger to the integrity of democratic institutions. In recent years we have seen a serious wedge driven into the political life of my country and several European countries. There is a direct link between tracking by the online ad industry and the polarization of democratic societies.

A study by a group of Facebook executives in 2018 reported that almost 2/3 of people who joined extremist groups on Facebook were directed there by recommendations from Facebook's algorithms. And where do these systems get the data that informs their algorithms? From tracking us.

Professor Hany Farid, an expert at the University of California, Berkeley, has said, *"They didn't set out to fuel misinformation and hate and divisiveness, but that's what the algorithms learned."*

- Tracking is also a national security threat. The Congress of the United States has asked U.S. intelligence agencies to study how information gleaned from online data collection may be used by hostile foreign governments to spy on individuals and on the activities of the security apparatus.

In April of 2021, a bipartisan group of U.S. Senators wrote, "This information [from adtech data] would be a goldmine for foreign intelligence services that could exploit it to inform and supercharge hacking, blackmail, and influence campaigns." They went on to say, "Few Americans realize that [adtech companies] are siphoning off and storing...data to compile exhaustive dossiers about them...we must understand the serious national security risks posed by the unrestricted sale of Americans' data to foreign companies and governments.'"

- Further, the whole practice of online tracking may itself be illegal. The online ad industry operates on a system called Real-time Bidding or RTB. RTB is the engine that drives the bulk of online advertising activity and it may itself be illegal under the terms of GDPR. As I mentioned earlier, RTB tracks and broadcasts peoples' online behavior and location tens of billions of times a day in Europe without the informed consent of the individuals involved. I'm no legal scholar but it's hard for me to understand how this can be reconciled with the intent of GDPR.

Next I want to talk about online ad fraud. While there are certainly fraudulent activities aimed at consumers online, when we speak of ad fraud we are generally generally speaking about fraud perpetrated on advertisers.

The total amount of money spent by online advertisers worldwide is reported to be about $400 billion (in 2022-BH). Ad fraud is probably costing marketers tens of billions annually.

In its simplest form, ad fraud is a type of crime in which criminals steal money from businesses. The businesses think they are buying advertising, but they are actually buying nothing.While there are dozens of types of ad fraud, much ad fraud falls into one of three buckets — fraudulent audiences, fraudulent websites, or fraudulent clicks.

The way fraudsters take advantage of the vulnerability of the system is often by creating fake websites, fake audiences, and fake clicks. Criminals use software strings, called bots, to produce fake audiences and fake clicks. According to web security company Barracuda Networks, in 2020 there was more traffic on the web from malignant bots than there was from human beings. I am grossly simplifying the types of ad fraud here because in many cases you need to be a computer scientist or a software engineer to understand how these criminals corrupt the system.

Exploiting the online advertising system is apparently remarkably simple. According to Hewlett Packard Enterprises, ad fraud has both the highest potential for profitability and the lowest barrier to entry of any form of online criminal activity.

Nobody knows the exact extent of ad fraud, but several credible organizations estimate worldwide ad fraud in the range of $60 to $80 billion. Juniper Research has estimated it at $68 billion. Ad Age magazine estimated it at 20% of online ad spending - about $80 billion today.The Association of National Advertisers in the U.S. estimated it variously at $81 billion and $120 billion.

Professor Roberto Cavazos, economist at the University of Baltimore who has studied business fraud for over 30 years said, "... the level of ad fraud is now staggering. The digital advertising sector has ... higher fraud rates than multi-trillion-dollar sectors."

Dr. Augustine Fou, an expert in online ad fraud, calculated that just one detected instance of fraud called "Fireball" could generate 30 billion fraudulent ad impressions a minute. He said, *"... fraud on such a massive scale is beyond belief."*

The World Federation of Advertisers has asserted that by 2025 ad fraud could become the second largest source of criminal income in the world, after drug trafficking.

Once again, there is a connection between ad fraud and tracking. According to experts, most of the fraud occurs in what is called programmatic advertising. Programmatic advertising is advertising bought and sold by computers. According to a report by the Incorporated Society of British Advertisers 80% of the websites participating in the programmatic ecosystem are quote "not premium." Not premium is a nice British way of saying crap. And where does the programmatic ecosystem compile the data that it uses to feed these "not premium" websites? From tracking.

You might ask yourself, "so if marketers are foolish enough to allow themselves to be cheated like this, why should we care?" I think the answer is frightening. No one knows where all this stolen money is going. It is possible that it may be funding the activities of organized crime around the world. It is possible that it may also be falling into the hands of governments hostile to our democratic principles who are using it to undermine governments that this Parliament represents.

Think about it. If you were a bad guy and you could easily steal billions of dollars with very little chance of being caught and virtually no consequences even if you were caught, why wouldn't you?

The advertising industry was tremendously successful for many decades finding appropriate targets for TV, radio, newspaper and magazine advertisers before tracking came along. But the online ad industry claims that tracking is an essential part of their business model and without tracking their business model would fall apart. I find this hard to believe. It is the equivalent of saying that online advertising is such a weak force that the only way it can survive is if it is allowed to spy on the public. It is hard to take this argument seriously coming from some of the most profitable corporations the world has ever known.

As I said at the beginning, advertising is necessary for the continued operation of the free web. But tracking is not. The problem is not advertising. The problem is tracking.

The problems that tracking has created are of a scale enormously greater than any benefit tracking may claim to provide. I firmly believe that we can continue to have online advertising that is profitable to media companies and successful for online advertisers of all sizes without the perilous consequences of tracking. We have a very simple but important question in front of us. Is protecting the dangerous practices of the adtech industry more important than protecting the privacy rights of citizens and the integrity of democratic institutions? I hope not.

Thank you very much for listening.

Bob Hoffman

Part Three

Mktg Stinx

Dyspeptic Skeptic

Many otherwise sensible people seem to possess an unhealthy and bewildering confidence in the practice of marketing. I'm afraid I don't share their enthusiasm. After over fifty years in and around the marketing and advertising industries, I find myself more skeptical than ever. I am happy to say that I know a few brilliant marketing people. But just a few.

There have been a number of big name companies who have entrusted hundreds of millions of dollars to me to help them sell their stuff. In order to do that I had to pretend to listen to marketing wisdom. I listened respectfully. Then I mostly ignored the marketing clichés and did it my way.

Of course, there were times they wouldn't let me do it my way. This involved months of research, and focus groups, and reports, and powerpoint presentations, and meetings about powerpoint presentations, and reports about meetings, and meetings about memos, and memos about reports about meetings. In other words, an undiluted, full-bodied, multi-disciplinary clusterfuck that invariably resulted in some horseshit about 'quality and value.'

This next section is my revenge. I've cherry-picked some stuff I've written about the foibles, failures and fecklessness of traditional marketing wisdom. I've compiled them here for my own entertainment and, hopefully, yours.

If there's any group of people in marketing world that I haven't offended yet, this next section ought to do the trick.

Marketers Are From Mars, Consumers Are From New Jersey

Marketers and consumers (and by consumers I mean, ya know, people) are from different worlds. Consumers are basically simple creatures with straightforward needs and easily observed behaviors. Marketers are complicated bastards with strange customs and mysterious rituals.

Marketers are taught not to think simply. In fact, the whole practice of marketing is based on the conviction that there are forces at work in the minds of consumers that only trained specialists (ya know, *us*) are qualified to interpret. Thinking simply has been beaten out of marketers.

You can't be taken seriously in any marketing or advertising organization if you suggest that the bulk of consumer behavior is perfectly obvious. You can't advance your career by speaking plainly and asserting the indisputable — that the reason most people buy a product is because it's cheaper, more familiar, tastier, prettier or simply more readily available.

That kind of thinking just won't cut it in today's world of professional complexity. Today you need to be at least a sidewalk sociologist and, even better, a para-psychiatrist to be taken seriously as a marketing professional. In fact, you need to think and speak in ways that no consumer in the history of civilization has ever thought or spoken. How marketers think and how consumers think couldn't be more different. Here's how marketers think:

>*How can I create engagement between consumers and my brand?*
>
>*How can I align the meaning of my brand with my target audience?*
>
>*How can I co-create with my target and develop a conversation?*

Here's how consumers think:

>*Will there be parking?*
>
>*Is there anyone here who knows what the hell he's talking about?*
>
>*Will this fucking thing work?*
>
>*How badly are they going to screw me?*

Consumers want clarity and simplicity. Marketers want to complicate the shit out of everything

Glossary of Marketing

Marketing people speak a language that is unsettling to the human ear, mystifying to the human mind, and an affront to the human soul.

To help you through this bewildering experience, I have created a glossary of terms that can help you understand what marketing people actually mean when they speak.

Glossary of Marketing Terminology

Content - *anything*

Branded content - *anything with a logo*

Compelling content - *content*

Storyteller - *copywriter*

Engage - *bother*

Brand architect - *marketing intern*

Authentic – *true-ish sounding*

Transparent – *true-ish looking*

Conversation - *retweet*

Follower – *online stranger who wants something from you*

Advisor - *LinkedIn term for unemployed*

Community – *online strangers who once clicked your link*

Branded - *having a logo*

Activation - *marketing people doing something*

Workshop - *meeting*

Roundtable - *meeting*

Summit - *meeting*

Town hall meeting - *meeting*

Training session - *powerpoint-induced napping opportunity*

Webinar - *powerpoint-induced napping opportunity on Zoom*

Traditional – *derogatory term by marketing people for anything they can't do well*

Brand advocate - *customer*

Brand ambassador - *customer*

Brand evangelist - *customer*

Data-driven - *unimaginative*

Brand purpose - *something the CEO's spouse is into*

Disruptive - s*omething the CEO's daughter is into*

Target audience - *people like us*

There are probably several other marketing terms you've come across that you didn't understand. Don't worry. We don't understand them either.

Robbie & Ruthie Talk About Pickles

The phone rings:

ROBBIE: Hello.

RUTHIE: Robert, it's your Aunt Ruthie.

ROBBIE: Hi Ruthie.

RUTHIE: Hello, darling.

ROBBIE: What's up?

RUTHIE: I'm calling to ask a favor.

ROBBIE: Sure.

RUTHIE: My pickles are selling very well, and Big Save says they'll put them in their supermarkets all across the country, but I have to do some advertising. So I thought as long as my nephew is a big-shot advertising man, maybe your company could make an ad for me.

ROBBIE: Sure.

RUTHIE: So here's what I want the ad to say... Aunt Ruthie's Pickles are homemade, they taste wonderful, and we use fresh ingredients.

ROBBIE: Well, okay, but we really need to think a little more about this.

RUTHIE: Um...okay...what?

ROBBIE: Well, first we need to understand the consumer.

RUTHIE: The consumer?

ROBBIE: It's a...a person who buys things.

RUTHIE: Everyone buys things.

ROBBIE: Right...

RUTHIE: So how is a consumer different from a person?

ROBBIE: Um...it's not.

RUTHIE: So why don't you just call it a person?

ROBBIE: Okay, so it's a person.

RUTHIE: Okay so you have to understand this...person. Why?

ROBBIE: So we can know how they use your product.

RUTHIE: They eat it. How else do you use a pickle?

ROBBIE: Well, yeah...but why do they eat it?

RUTHIE: Because it tastes good. (PAUSE) Robbie, are you okay?

ROBBIE: I'm fine. You see, we have to analyze who we should be talking to in our advertising. We call that a target audience. Should we talk to women 18-49 or men 25-34 or...?

RUTHIE: Why don't we just talk to people who buy pickles?

ROBBIE: Well you see, the perception of your brand has to resonate...

RUTHIE: My what?

ROBBIE: Your brand...it's the essence of your product...

RUTHIE: My pickles have an essence?

ROBBIE: It's like their personality

RUTHIE: My pickles have a personality?

ROBBIE: Well, it's not the pickles that have the personality, it's you, it's Aunt Ruthie's ...

RUTHIE: My personality? I'm a pain in the ass. What the hell does anyone care about my personality?

ROBBIE: But Aunt Ruthie is your brand .

RUTHIE: I thought Aunt Ruthie was my name .

ROBBIE: And your name is your brand

RUTHIE: So why don't you just call it my name?

ROBBIE: Let's look at it this way - what is your brand purpose?

RUTHIE: Excuse me?

ROBBIE: Why do Aunt Ruthie's Pickles exist?

RUTHIE: They exist so I can make some money and pay off that French piece of shit car I bought you...

ROBBIE: No, I mean what do they mean to the world?

RUTHIE: They don't mean shit. They just taste good (PAUSE) Robert, why are you talking like this? Are you having that trouble you had back in college?

ROBBIE: You know I've committed to never doing that again...

RUTHIE: So why are you talking like this? Is this how you talk in your company?

ROBBIE: Well, yes. You see, Aunt Ruthie, we believe advertising isn't only about selling your pickles. It's about developing a conversation between your brand and the consumer by having transparent communication that creates advocates by over-delivering on brand expectations and creating relevant brand experiences that emphasize the essential purpose your brand brings to the world...

RUTHIE: You know, honey, your cousin Stanley majored in English, maybe I'll just ask him to write the ad...

ROBBIE: No, no....I'll...

RUTHIE: Robbie, darling, you know I love you, right? And I would never say anything to hurt you. But listen to me, darling. You people are crazy.

Click

Stop Branding

Branding is a made-up word about an imaginary activity. Successful brands are not built by 'branding.' They are built by doing a lot of *other* things right.

Some objectives can only be achieved indirectly. You can't be happy by *trying* to be happy. The way to be happy is to appreciate what you have, and help other people. You can't have a happy marriage by *trying* to have a happy marriage. The way to have a happy marriage is to stop whining, and clean up after yourself.

It's the same with brands. Successful brands are created indirectly. The way to have a successful brand is…

> …make a high quality product
>
> …take good care of your customers
>
> …distinctive product and package design
>
> …consistency in price and distribution
>
> …do advertising that makes you famous.

You want to build a successful brand? Stop 'branding.' Do your other jobs right and a strong brand will be a pleasant by-product.

Is It Art or Science?

One of the interesting questions about advertising that I have tried to explore from time to time is whether we should think of it more as art or science.

With the growth in the use of technology, mathematics, metrics, and data it appears that certain aspects of advertising are becoming more scientific. However, I am not convinced that advertising as a whole is any more scientific.

From a practical standpoint, there is one factor that differentiates art from science. In science, there is an "arrow of progress." Science points in a direction and gets progressively more specific and effectual.

If you buy a new car, it is more likely to last longer, be safer, work more reliably, and be more efficient than it was fifty years ago. If you have high blood pressure today, you are more likely to be successfully treated for it than you would have been fifty years ago. If you have a personal computer, it can do more things, more effectively, more quickly and more reliably than it did fifty...wait a minute...we didn't have personal computers fifty years ago. The point is, science provides us with technological progress by degrees that builds on itself and improves stuff.

Art, on the other hand, does not have an arrow of progress. It's not supposed to. Art is about human interpretation – emotions and aesthetics – not ongoing improvements. You want to improve on Mona Lisa? Good luck.

There is no way to talk about whether the work of Picasso represents "progress" from DaVinci. You may prefer one to the other, but to speak about progress is meaningless. Similarly, is there an arrow of progress from Beethoven to James Brown? Or Shakespeare to Updike? One may certainly have influenced the other, and styles certainly change, but talking about improvement is moot.

That doesn't mean art isn't inventive or innovative. Or that older forms don't influence newer forms. It just means that art moves unsystematically and, unlike science, we don't judge new art based on having improved upon old art.

So the question of whether advertising should be considered more science than art rests on answering this question: Is there an arrow of progress? In other words, is advertising more effective and more successful at its objectives than it used to be?

Exploring the literature of advertising over the past ten years, one would have to conclude that advertising is *less* effective, not more. The literature is rife with assertions and research that conclude that advertising's effectiveness seems to have diminished over time.

There are certain aspects of advertising that claim to utilize scientific principles more effectively – media planning, programmatic buying – but there isn't much in the way of conclusive evidence to support the idea that advertising as a whole has gotten more effective.

In fact, despite all the hoo-hah over the precision targeting of online advertising, behavioral targeting seems to be only marginally more effective than no targeting at all. It is not clear that when the marginal positive effect of behavioral targeting appears, it is even due to the effects of advertising. It may well be that the reason behavioral targeting sometimes appears to be more effective is simply that the people whose purchasing is being reported on have been so carefully pinpointed that they are the most likely people for buying the product, regardless of advertising. Economists call this the "selection effect." The selection effect posits that the appearance of more effective advertising can be a mirage that is caused by the targeting of people who were already more likely to buy, click, or download your product.

But even if we stipulate that certain aspects of advertising have become more scientific, I would still contend that the overarching goal of advertising – the creation of successful brands – is no nearer to a scientific practice than it was when I entered the advertising business thousands of years ago.

From what I can see, despite all the technological advances we have applied and all the words that have been written, we have uncovered no new generally accepted principles about the nature of brand building or consumer behavior. Most marketers are still thrashing around in the dark trying to either build a brand or maintain one.

Regardless of the growing veneer of scientific processes, there seems to be no arrow of progress that has helped us create more successful advertising.

Women With Their Shirts Off

I had a feeling that headline would get your attention.

A long time ago Adweek magazine asked me to write something for them. The premise was this: They would take two ads in the same category -- one contemporary and one from a million years ago -- and have an expert (that's me!) evaluate the ads to see which was better.

They wanted the piece to be provocative, so they chose the bra category. Now, honestly, I'm not really a professional on the subject of bras. But I do like to think of myself as a talented amateur.

The two facing ads are the ones they provided me. My comments to Adweek are below the pictures.

MAIDENFORM VS. VICTORIA'S SECRET

Despite the fact that the woman in the Maidenform ad…

...has a Mickey Mouse hairdo

…is holding the pool cue like a cigar

…has cups so alarmingly pointy they could cause permanent damage to some dumb bastard just trying to cop a feel, the Maidenform ad is about a thousand times better than the Victoria's Secret ad.

You see, back in the 1960's when the Maidenform ad ran, advertising had a secret ingredient. That secret ingredient was called a "concept." A concept was an idea about a product that was at the core of every ad. The concept for the Maidenform campaign was expressed in this line of copy: "I dreamed I *(DID SOMETHING)* in my Maidenform bra."

Now let's be honest here. It was a silly concept. Silly and mildly scandalous. The silliness was forgiven by the "dream" contrivance. The scandalousness was a little more subtle. It wasn't the first time America saw a model in a bra. But it may have been the first time we saw a model in a bra in a social situation.

What made the campaign so powerful was exactly this juxtaposition of incongruities. The campaign, I believe, was enormously successful. It achieved the most important thing advertising can do: It made them famous. In today's dreadful parlance it had great 'cultural currency' and became part of 'the conversation' (god forgive me.) I can almost hear Johnny Carson cracking wise about it.

The Victoria's Secret ad, on the other hand, has absolutely nothing going for it. It is a generic ad, featuring a model — she's probably some super- famous super-model I've never heard of -- in a coquettish pose that looks like a zillion other super-models in coquettish poses. The typography is virtually unreadable. And it lacks the one thing that differentiates an ad from a catalog page – that quaint old thing called a concept.

The Maidenform ad was unmistakable. The Victoria's Secret ad is unrecognizable. And that, my friend, is the difference between great advertising and average advertising.

By the way, I learned something from this exercise. When I was growing up in New York City there was a girl in our neighborhood we used to call "pencil tits." She looked like she had two pencils standing up in her sweater. I finally know how she got that look.

The Restaurant for People Who Don't Like Food

I don't want to be a salesman. I want to be an artist. I want to change the world. I've seen the damage that crass consumerism can do. I don't want to be a peddler. I am nobler than that. You know what I mean, right? You agree, right?

Well, here's the thing. If you're in marketing or advertising you're a salesman. It doesn't matter what you *think* you are or what you *want* to be. You're a salesman. I don't like it either.

One of the problems advertising has always faced is that there are a lot of people in the business who don't want to be salespeople. They have a vested interest — a personal, self-image interest — in not thinking of themselves as salespeople. And today they have more opportunity than ever to act on this delusion.

They have convinced themselves, and many others in the marketing industry, that selling is not the purpose of advertising. They go to conferences and write books and make presentations that tell us that the nature of consumer behavior has changed. That selling is no longer our goal. That 'brand purpose' is our true raison d'etre.

They don't want to make ads. Ads are too graceless, too direct, and too transparently commercial. Everyone knows the motives behind ads. They'd rather do their work behind an opaque curtain. They'd rather make believe that what they're doing is a contribution to social justice. It makes them feel better. They're not here to sell you something. They want to have a conversation and build a win-win relationship.

They can cling to their timid, anemic illusions all they want but in the end they will be judged on how good they are at selling. Sorry, amigo, that's business.

In my hometown of Oakland, California, there's a restaurant I hate. It's very chic and popular with a certain type of person – a person who likes restaurants but doesn't like food.

Everything about it is unappetizing. It has a cheerless austerity that appeals to the guilty wealthy. The food is very artfully arranged twigs and pebbles. It's as if the chef learned his craft working with Tinker Toys. They are afraid to use any ingredient that might add flavor to one of their precious concoctions, as it might also taint its virtue.

Today we have agencies like this. They are agencies for people who don't like advertising. They are post-advertising agencies. They have no interest in the art, no passion for the craft. They have no zeal for selling. They tell us that today's human does not want to be sold to. As if any human ever did.

They want to co-create, and have conversations, and share values. Everything about these agencies is unappetizing. They, too, have a cheerless austerity. They believe that persuasion is an insult to their relationship with the consumer. They believe that selling will taint their virtue. They are bloodless, timid, and unenthusiastic.

Not me. I like selling. I like persuasion. I like advertising. I like food.

Life in Conferenceland

One of the downsides of making your living as a professional loudmouth is that you have to do it in public. That means participating in conferences. As everyone knows, there's nothing in the world as dreary as a marketing conference, with the possible exception of an SEO webinar or lunch with a yoga maniac.

It is my good fortune that when I speak at conferences I am usually billed as the keynote, which often means I get to speak first. Speaking first has one great advantage. After I speak I can wait until no one's looking then sneak out the back door and find a nice quiet bar.

I was at a conference a few months ago and I decided to be mature and hang around and listen to some other speakers. I'll never make that mistake again. Here's what I learned:

- The future is going to be amazing. No one's going to have to do anything. Everything will be done for us by AI, or robots, or Jeff Bezos. We won't have to work, rotate our tires, or chew our food.

- AI, by the way, will be stealing our jobs, our airline miles, and our children.

- Women will also be amazing. When they run everything there will be no poverty or inequality or wait times at the Genius Bar. One exception: that nutty jailbird from Theranos.

- Advertising, on the other hand, is not amazing. In fact, it's dead. It's going to be replaced by the metaverse or NFTs or blockchain or something.

- Better expect the unexpected because if you expect the expected than your expectations will be unexpectedly...I don't know...something very scary.

- China and India are going to have their own internets which will be better than ours because your password will be embedded in your brain or your kidneys and you won't have to update Adobe every half hour.

- Data is not only the secret to marketing success, it also makes your car's engine run smoother and – something you probably didn't know – it makes a great Father's Day gift!

- Facebook is changing. No, really, they mean it this time! They're going to be double-extra careful with our data, our bank account numbers, and our drug bust records by taking all our files and putting them in Ziploc bags. And if anyone tries to break into them they will suspend them and not let them open another Facebook account for almost twenty minutes. Unless they use another name.

- Consumers love your brand and want a relationship with it and want to join the conversation about it and share it with their tribe... or, wait a minute... (DISSOLVE TO 30 MINUTES LATER)... brands mean nothing to consumers. The internet has disintermediated everything and the whole idea of brands is totally stupid and obsolete... (CUT TO PANEL DISCUSSION)

- Gen Z is a whole new species of human that is even cooler than millennials. You have to get rid of all those idiot millennials because they are stupid dinosaurs. If you don't have a Gen Z strategy in place by tomorrow 9 am you are already too late and you are dead. By the way, we are holding a 3-day Gen Z Insider Summit in Orlando next month...

- Consumers will love your brand of peanut milk even more if your brand purpose aligns with their values and they know you are committed to world peace and single-payer pet burials.

- And, by the way, everything is changing and if your business doesn't transform you will be left behind and die. It doesn't matter what you are, you have to transform into something else. It doesn't matter what you transform into as long as you stop doing whatever it is you are doing and start doing something that requires AI, robots, or Jeff Bezos.

Bottom line: The only sensible reason for attending a marketing conference is to get as far away as possible from the dreary reality of marketing itself. Like Disneyland, marketing's Conferenceland is much cleaner, prettier, and safer than the actual thing.

My advice is stay the hell away from marketing conferences unless, of course, I'm speaking. In which case, bring the whole family.

Legend of Marketing Man

Basically, there are two types of men – Feckless Weasels and Smelly Hairballs.

Your classic Feckless Weasel lives in Portland, drives a Subaru Outback, spends 80% of his time trying to please his shrill harridan of a wife, and wastes the other 20% 'reasoning' with his horrid children ("Now, Joshie, remember we said in a restaurant we don't put our feet in other peoples' food...")

The Smelly Hairball, on the other hand, has old banana peels in his golf bag, is at least three months behind in his alimony, has an expired driver's license, and is quite fond of the phrase "SHUT THE FUCK UP!"

In the rich pageant of manhood there is, sadly, very little fertile ground between the Feckless Weasel and the Smelly Hairball. There is, however, one exception – Marketing Man.

Marketing Man is an imaginary character (or as we like to call him, a 'target audience') who exists mainly in briefing documents. Marketing Man is handsome and well-groomed. He is thoughtful and considerate. He is a close shaver. He coaches soccer and is concerned with his wife's feelings. He is helpful in the kitchen and undemanding in the bedroom. He keeps his closet neat and his weenie in his pants. In other words, he's a dork.

Marketing Man now has an online place all to himself where he can gather with other Marketing Men and have conversations about...oh, I don't know...baking?

It's a super-slick website called "Man of the House" sponsored by Procter & Gamble. It's billed as *"...a man's guide to grooming, gadgets, fitness, relationships, clothes, parenting, careers & home repair."* In other words, everything that makes contemporary life such a pile of shit (couldn't they put in a *little* something about weed, guitars, and strippers? Just a *little*?)

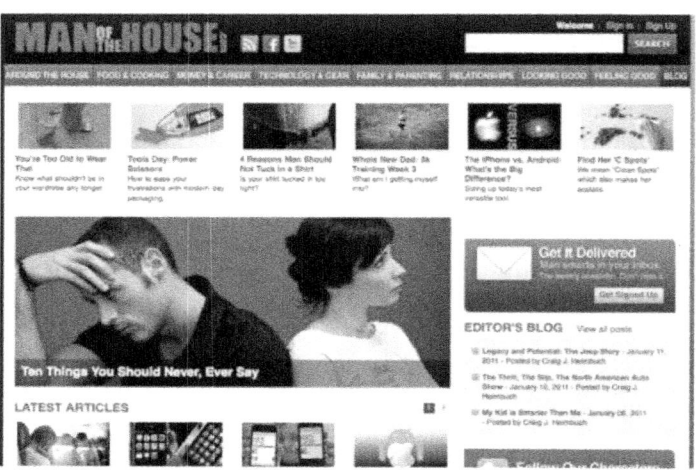

You are not going to believe this but I swear it's true -- here are some of the things you can read this week at the Man Of The House website:

- *Tips for Surviving a Weekend at Disney*
- *What Does Your Wife Want From You?*
- *Four Reasons Not To Tuck Your Shirt In*
- *How to Clean a Toilet in 30 Seconds Flat*
- *And great tips on having a Family Pizza Party*

Hemingway is spinning.

Note: I just checked and "Man of the House" no longer exists. Apparently, nothing can survive a Weekend at Disney.

Simplifiers and Complicators

There are two kinds of business people: people who simplify things and people who complicate them. In most businesses, complicators are annoying. In advertising they are ruinous.

Every time you create an ad there are a million things to say about the brand or product. One of the keys to producing a successful ad is in understanding what is essential and what is extraneous. Simplifiers have the ability to cut down the weeds and clear a path. Complicators cannot distinguish between the pertinent and the irrelevant.

If you're working with a planner or a creative director who is a complicator, you understand the frustration involved. If you're working with a client who's a complicator, you're probably thinking about accepting that fry job at Burger King.

In an ad agency or a marketing department one highly placed complicator can undo the good work of a dozen simplifiers.

Industrialization of Advertising

It's obvious that the structure of the advertising business has changed in recent years. Not quite so obvious is that the *nature* of the business has also changed. Advertising has become industrialized.

A business becomes "industrialized" when it is optimized for efficiency over craftsmanship.

If you're making commodity products -- pencils, nail clippers, shoe laces, cars -- optimizing for efficiency can be an excellent business strategy. Money is saved and once a satisfactory template is created, reproducing thousands of copies is economical and advantageous.

It's a little different, however, when you're selling a service that is intended to be uniquely individual. In that case, optimizing efficiency over craftsmanship can have bad results.

I don't think I'm being unfair when I say that the quality of advertising has gotten worse in recent years. Substantially worse. What I have found in my recent travels is that this is also true of our media strategies. Off the record chats with executives in media have opened my eyes to the fact that they, too, feel they are being pressed for efficiency over craftsmanship.

Imagined efficiencies are the drivers of programmatic buying. The fact that programmatic is notoriously dodgy and wasteful is not lost on agency media people. But agency management knows that turning buys over to a shady mechanized process is a type of 'efficiency' you can defend and monetize.

You have to credit the media agencies - and the entire agency business - for their ability to hide the true costs of their efficiencies from their clients. Among all the scandals, improprieties, and damaging revelations that the press has uncovered about adtech and online advertising, has there been *even one* that has been exposed by an agency? That's what ya call a rhetorical question because the answer is a big flaming no.

It's not surprising that this has happened. When customers demand all- you-can-eat at reduced prices; when investors demand high returns regardless of circumstances; when good enough is the standard unit of quality, it is inevitable that craftsmanship will take a back seat.

There are several manifestations of industrialization apparent in the ad industry now.

- First is consolidation. A tiny number of organizations control an enormous amount of the market.

- Next is the ascendancy of online advertising. Because programmatic buying rides on a bed of technology, it has the appearance of efficiency. The fact that much of it is wildly inefficient is of little consequence. It is a very useful tool by which industrialized agencies can be profitable without paying for expensive craftspeople, and with little danger of clueless clients understanding what's actually going on.

- People both inside and outside the ad business believe that the quality of advertising has gotten worse. A recent study showed that compared to 20 years ago, twice as many people said they found advertising annoying.

- Talented people don't want to work in advertising. According to the ANA *"We're having a talent crisis, meaning there is not a shortage of talented professionals as much as a broader industry failure to convince them that full-time advertising roles are worth taking."*

It's clear that the leaders of the ad industry - regardless of disingenuous pronouncements to the contrary - are satisfied with the state of things. The best thing that could happen to the advertising business would be for clients to suddenly demand craftsmanship. Ain't holdin' my breath.

Sell More Shit

I was sitting in a client meeting. The client was talking to us about doing a new campaign. One of my agency MBA geniuses asked the client the question they always ask when they have nothing to contribute and want to sound engaged, "What is your objective for this campaign?"

I passed him a note: "Please see me after the meeting."

An hour later he was sitting in my office. "Did you ever see one of those TV spots for investment houses where they say 'we'll review your investment goals and design a plan? '" I said.

"Yes," he said.

"Well, here's a secret. Everyone in the world has the same investment goal -- make more money . There's never been an investor who didn't have that goal. They may *say* they have a different goal, or they may have a fancy name for it, but their goal is always the same. Make more money. You see what I'm saying?"

"Um... I guess so."

"Let me clarify." I said. "Telling people that you will review their investment goals, is the same as saying 'I'm a fucking idiot' because if you don't understand that everyone's investment goal is to make more money you have to be a fucking idiot. Do you understand now?"

"Oh, okay, yes."

"Now," I said, "how does that relate to our meeting this morning?"

"I don't know."

"Okay, I'm going to reveal to you now the amazing secret of advertising. Every client in the world has the same objective – sell more shit. There's never been a client who didn't have that goal. Repeat after me – their objective is to sell more shit."

"Their objective is to sell more shit."

"Good. Now, if I ever hear you ask a client what her objective is again, I will fire you. Every client and every campaign in the world has the same objective. The objective is...you tell me. "

"Sell more shit."

"Bingo! Meeting over."

Asking The Wrong Questions

Any agency person who's ever participated in a new business pitch has been asked this question: "What is the process you use to develop advertising ideas?"

Every agency person mentally answered this way, "Schmuck, there is no process." No one ever said that out loud.

There may be a process for developing a strategy; there may be a process for developing a media plan; but there is no process for giving birth to an idea. There never has been and there never will be.

Nonetheless, when asked the question, the agency usually trots out a chart with arrows and boxes and buckets and silos and feedback loops and checkpoints and all manner of obfuscatory baloney. The chart usually has a very pompous sounding title, like *'Developmental Matrix'* and it shows how through psychographic analysis the idea starts as a small spark of insight and then by some highly evolved system it is inflated into a grand unifying concept.

In other words, it's a full seven-course bullshit banquet.

How it really happens is like this: a writer and art director are locked in a cage. A creative director opens the cage door just wide enough to throw in 5 pounds of briefing documents, memos, research reports, and old ads. He slams the door, yells *"I need this shit by Thursday, and it better be fucking good"* and runs off to lunch with his assistant.

How do you like the process now, amigo?

The Invisible Advertising Awards

I would like to start a new way to think about advertising awards. I would like to recognize an ignored and under-appreciated minority -- the unseen people who say no to terrible ideas.

Having spent hundreds of years in the advertising business, there is no doubt in my mind that the advertising and marketing industries generate far more bad ideas that never get produced than good ideas that get produced.

This is why we have creative directors. Someone has to separate the wheat from the shit. As a former creative director myself, I would estimate that for every ad I approved I turned down about 10 (I'm sure some of my former colleagues will get a good hearty chuckle from that estimate, but for the sake of this essay, and in the spirit of generosity, let's assume I wasn't quite as big a prick as they might claim.)

The point I'm trying to make is that if the ratio of bad to good is somewhere near ten to one, there is a very large gap in our appreciation of the importance of saying no.

We celebrate the people who create good ideas, but we do not celebrate the people with the good sense to save us from the bad ones. And yet, bad ideas may have as much potential to do harm as good ones have to do good.

Imagine if someone at Pepsi had quietly said no to the Kendall Jenner monstrosity of a few years ago. That person would have invisibly delivered an enormous benefit to Pepsi, but would never have been recognized for it. The invisible person would never be known, no less win an award, but would have contributed mightily.

So let's just take a minute to thank all the brilliant, brave, and invisible people who, in the face of often strident and self-righteous opposition, have the good sense and large balls to say no to stupid ideas.

Then, of course, there is the other kind of invisible excellence. It is the wonderful work of highly talented people that does not get approved. Among the ranks of the aforementioned creative directors, there is no shortage of imbeciles. As anyone who has ever worked in business is surely aware, a highly-placed idiot can kill or cripple the excellent work of dozens of good people.

A good deal of excellent, award-worthy work gets killed every year by the arbitrary stupidity of dimwits (once again, I'm sure some of my former underlings are getting a good chuckle from that but, again in the spirit of generosity, let's assume I wasn't quite as big a moron as they might claim.) The result is that there appears to be a much smaller pool of excellent ideas than there actually is. I think there's a term for this called "survival bias." In other words, we believe there isn't much excellent work being done because only a fraction of it survives. The excellent work that gets killed or mutilated is invisible.

Imagine all the good ideas for Pepsi that must have died so that Kendall Jenner could live. It is my belief that the invisible marketing and advertising contributions are at least as important to our industry as the visible contributions. The only problem is, um, they're invisible.

So to all the talented, sensible, and invisible people who contributed to our industry this year by saving us from bad ideas, and to the creatively excellent people with wonderful ideas that suffered ignominious dismemberment at the hands of nitwits, thank you.

This essay is your award.

Advertising's Hidden Enemy

The advertising and marketing industries had a dream. The dream was that interactive media would revolutionize advertising and make it far more engaging, relevant, and effective. There's been a problem. Nobody's interested in interacting with advertising. In fact, one of the greatest benefits to consumers of interactivity is that it helps them *avoid* advertising.

Historically, interactivity has been the enemy of advertising. TV advertising became less effective with the invention of the remote. It was a lot more effective when people had to drag their asses off the sofa to change the channel. Radio advertising became less effective with the invention of the car push-button radio. As soon as an ad came on people interacted. Today the ability to click away, or scroll past a display ad, or the ability to click "skip ad" on YouTube is a pleasure for consumers, and a toothache for advertisers. Interactivity helps people avoid advertising.

Click through rates on display ads continue to drop. By most reports they are below one in a thousand. Every attempt at "interactive" TV has been a dismal failure. YouTube has billions of ostensibly "viral" videos. The overwhelmingly majority of which have never been viewed by anyone but the creator's mom.

Of course, we never hear or read about any of this. The narratives we are exposed to about marketing activities and the beliefs we have in the success of these activities are profoundly skewed by the bias toward trumpeting success, not failure.

What marketers seem unable to comprehend is that, at best, advertising is a minor annoyance. It is pretty clear that most people are willing to go to substantial lengths to avoid it. Streaming video now constitutes a significant part of all TV viewing. Much of it costs people up to $100 a year, but part of the value proposition is that it's largely ad free.

Easy interaction with a medium is not an advertiser's friend. But there is apparently no end to marketers' ability to delude themselves. And also no end to ad hustlers' willingness to feed these delusions.

There are a few exceptions. Happily there are some very talented people in advertising who can create ads that are so interesting, beautiful, or funny that people will not try to avoid them. Unhappily, there ain't many of them.

For the most part, the only way to get most people to pay attention to your advertising message is to force them to do it. This is why social media marketing - which started life with a utopian vision of free "sharing" and "conversations" - quickly evolved into traditional paid advertising. Mr. Zuckerberg thanks you.

The lovely fantasy of online advertising -- in which the same person who was frantically clicking her remote to escape from TV advertising was going to merrily click her mouse to interact with online advertising -- is going to go down as one of the great marketing delusions of all time. It has been undermined by an unfortunate fact of nature -- no one in his right mind volunteers for advertising.

By a factor of about a thousand to one, people who can interact with media do so to avoid advertising -- not engage with it.

Creativity Without Talent

Someone once asked me about a copywriter who had worked for me. "Is he creative?" the person asked. "Very" I replied, "and it's a shame because he's not very talented."

I, too, am burdened with this frustrating affliction -- more creativity than talent. I spend an inordinate amount of time writing and playing musical instruments. I love doing these things. But, alas, I'm just not very good at them. I have written some decent ads, some pretty good blog posts, and some fairly lousy songs. Yes, I create a lot of stuff. But no one would accuse me of being terribly talented.

But this isn't about me, it's about advertising. We are often confronted with the lament that advertising isn't very good. This is true, and one of the reasons it's true is that the ad industry is chock full of people like me. I've seen them from all sides. As a copywriter, I've worked alongside them. As a creative director I've supervised them. As an agency head, I've recruited them. They are hard-working, diligent, and well-meaning. Unfortunately, they're not very talented.

By definition, the average creative person is average. And as George Carlin would remind us, half of them are below average. We often blame the absence of excellence in advertising on tin-eared clients, unimaginative strategies, or weak-kneed account work. The truth, however, is a little more complicated — it ain't easy. Talent is a rare and precious thing.

It's not that we don't want to do great work. It's not that we don't try to do great work. It's just that great work is really, really difficult to do. It takes exceptional talent, and sadly, exceptional talent is the exception.

Here's to the Bobbleheads

Here's to the bobbleheads.

Here's to the ones who sit at every meeting and nod in agreement.

Here's to the ones who never have a dangerous idea or an oddball opinion.

Here's to the ones who always agree with the highest ranking person in the room.

Here's to the ones who go to conferences and tweet out the banalities.

Here's to the guys and gals who start every sentence with, "Consumers told us…"

Here's to the ones who think their job is to make someone happy.

Here's to the ones who have no questions.

Here's to the ones who agree with the last person they spoke to.

Here's to the ones who produce the biggest decks and the fuzziest briefs.

Here's to the ones who can't finish a sentence without saying "disrupt" or "journey."

Here's to the ones who know all of the platitudes and none of the facts.

Here's to the true believers — the new kings and queens of marketing.

Here's to the bobbleheads!

The Existential Adman

Before we get into this, let's acknowledge that "*The Existential Adman*" is the worst title for an essay in the history of ad jabbering. But we soldier on unafraid...

Why do we care about marketing or advertising? Is there anything in it worthy of our attention and concern? These are the existential questions that I hope to answer in this essay.

Let's start with a wide shot and then cut to the extreme close-up. The wide shot is this: Is there anything *anywhere* worth caring about?

To contemplate this we need to get a sense of our place in the universe. We hear a lot of awe-inspiring horseshit from pop-TV gasbags about the 100's of billions of stars in a galaxy and the hundreds of billions of galaxies in the universe. This gives us the impression that the universe is teeming with stuff.

In fact, the universe is the emptiest thing you can imagine. Only 0.00000000000000000004 percent of the universe contains any matter. The universe has less actual substance than a social media pitch deck.

Our planet is not even a speck of dust on a galactic scale. On a universal scale it essentially doesn't exist. Still worried about whether your socks match?

The next depressing reality concerns our species. Our planet has been around for about 4 billion years. We homo sapiens have been here for about 300,000 years. So what portion of the Earth's life have we been a part of? The answer again is a decimal point and a lot of zeroes, -- .00008 to be exact.

In other words, our stay here at The Planet Earth Inn and Suites has been quite a short one and, sadly, promises not to last very much longer. The chances of us blowing ourselves up, melting ourselves down, or poisoning ourselves seem to be growing daily.

So the question is, if we are so insignificant and so temporary does *anything* really matter? This philosopher believes that no, nothing really matters. But in order to live an orderly life we have to *pretend* it matters. If we don't *pretend* things matter, we're all likely to wind up in the gutter drugged up and filthy. You remember college, right?

Next we get to marketing and advertising. In light of all this meaninglessness and nothingness how can anyone take this stuff seriously? Well, first of course, there's the money. We gotta pay for Netflix somehow. But let's be honest. There's something fascinating about what we do that transcends payday. Studying this stuff helps us strip away some of the fanciful notions of human rectitude, and more often than not exposes the depth of human venality to those of us who are willing to recognize it.

Of course there are those in our business who, despite all evidence to the contrary, believe that peoples' purchasing habits are motivated by high-minded principles and not by utter self-indulgence. But to those of us with feet planted firmly here on planet Earth, marketing and advertising present a unique lens through which we can view human behavior in a way that is not always evident in other lines of endeavor.

And now for the existential answers: Does this stuff mean anything? No. But is it interesting? Yes.

No Wonder Mktg Stinx

An article in MarketingWeek gave us a pretty good indication of why so much marketing is so awful.

According to a study conducted by Deloitte, *"functional marketing knowledge is considered only the sixth most useful skill"* among marketing executives.

Imagine if 'functional medical knowledge' was considered only the sixth most useful skill among doctors. Or if 'functional flying knowledge' was considered only the sixth most useful skill among pilots. Or if 'functional toilet knowledge' was the sixth most useful skill among plumbers?

Is it any wonder so much marketing is such a pile of crap?

What do these clowns think their job is? According to the article, these people think the three most important traits for a marketer are being *"communicative, collaborative and resilient."*

These people don't want to be marketers. They want to be cruise ship greeters.

Acknowledgements

Big thanks to Jeff Goodby for designing the cover (insider tip: feed Goodby a couple of glasses of wine and he'll do *anything!*).

Further thanks to Dr. Krzysztof Franaszek who inadvertently provided a lot of the research that went into creating this thing.

As always, thanks to Dr. Augustine Fou and Don Marti, people who understand how computer technology is used (and abused) and don't mind struggling to make it partially understandable to a dumb-ass copywriter.

Finally, thanks to some people who, perhaps without knowing it, have influenced my thinking about how advertising, media, and marketing actually work - Dave Trott, Paul Feldwick, Rory Sutherland, Byron Sharp, Mark Ritson, Dr. Karen Nelson-Field, and Brian Jacobs.

I'm sure every one of these people disagrees with some of the cockamamie ideas in this book, so don't blame them.

About The Author

Bob Hoffman has written six previous books about advertising that were Amazon #1 sellers.

He is a retired advertising executive who served as chief executive of three agencies.

In 2021, Bob was asked to speak to members of the British Parliament. In 2023, he was invited to Brussels to speak at the European Parliament.

Bob has spoken about advertising in twenty-four countries.

He lives in Oakland, California.

Printed in Great Britain
by Amazon

52186954R00138